ORIENTAL FORTUNE TELLING

ORIENTAL
FORTUNE TELLING

by Jimmei Shimano

translated by Togo Taguchi

CHARLES E. TUTTLE COMPANY
Rutland, Vermont & Tokyo, Japan

Representatives

For Continental Europe:
BOXERBOOKS, INC., Zurich

For the British Isles:
PRENTICE-HALL INTERNATIONAL, INC., London

For Australasia:
BOOK WISE (AUSTRALIA) PTY. LTD.
104-108 Sussex Street, Sydney 2000

Published by the Charles E. Tuttle Company, Inc.
of Rutland, Vermont & Tokyo, Japan
with editorial offices at Suido 1-chome, 2–6, Bunkyo-ku
Tokyo, Japan

© 1956 by Charles E. Tuttle Co., Inc.

Library of Congress Catalog
Card No. 65–18960

International Standard Book No. 0-8048-0448-6

First printing, 1965
Eleventh printing, 1981

Typography and book design by
Keiko Chiba

Printed in Japan

Foreword

Yi augury tells cycles of good and bad luck

HAVE you ever thought of the mysterious tide of luck that carries you willy-nilly despite your own intentions?

At vital moments in your life—when starting on a new business, or making an important decision—what you need most is advice from friends, seniors, and others with much experience, sensibility and wisdom.

You may not need their advice when you are in a happy state, full of confidence in yourself.

But you cannot expect to be in such a state at all times, and heaven knows what misfortune may befall you just when you are reaching the height of your success. It might be a tragic accident or illness, or a business failure due to an economic recession, or a serious mistake in negotiations, or a misunderstanding in human relations. Such misfortunes may happen to you because you are subject to a cycle of good and bad luck.

A man taking pride in his robust health may suddenly contract a fatal disease, and a long-time pauper may suddenly come into riches.

Just as there are business cycles in the economy, so are there alternating periods of good and bad luck in the life of everyone.

A seemingly happy man who has never known any want of money may have a hidden complex about his fate, which, he vaguely knows, is beyond his control.

When you are at the bottom of your cycle of luck, there is no use struggling to go up, for you will merely bog down deeper.

At such moments, it would be far better to stay just where you are, grasping whatever straw you may find within reach to keep your head above water and catch a breath, waiting until you recover enough strength to ride upward on the next surge of your luck.

Yi augury tells you when the next wave of your luck is forthcoming, and helps you immeasurably in making up your mind about whatever problem or doubt you may have.

A history of three thousand years in China

Three millenniums ago, the ancient Chinese developed Yi augury on the basis of what they saw and experienced in life. Starting with two basic elements—positive and negative, representing "Heaven" and "Earth" respectively—they divided all things in the universe into 11,520 forms, covering everything from celestial and earthly phenomena to architecture, agriculture, human affairs, and art. These were grouped into 64 types (subdivided into 384 variations), and each was represented by a combination of elements, which stood for a particular kind of possibility in life. The whole system of augury based on this theory was compiled into the *Book of Changes (Yi King)*, a philosophical work as well as the sacred book for all Yi augurs. It was completed through the efforts of one of the four greatest sages of the world,

Confucius, and supplemented by another wise man of the Orient, Mencius (B.C. 372–289).

Four new methods of divination

To the modern mind, augury may appear somewhat outmoded and impractical. Indeed, many people who have had disappointing experiences with irresponsible fortunetellers on the street are inclined to think that Yi augury has at best only a fifty-fifty chance of telling the truth. But it must be admitted that there is now a world-wide revival of interest in Yi augury, and that more and more people are coming to believe that this form of fortune telling based on the 3,000-year-old philosophy of the *Book of Changes* can be used effectively in the life of any sensible man living in the twentieth century.

If you turn to Yi augury when you are unlucky, the answer it provides will reflect your unlucky state and seldom predict an immediate happy turn. But you can draw a useful guide from what it tells you, and learn how soon your luck will return—how long you will have to wait before you enter the next upward phase of your cycle of luck.

The present book is intended to help you do just that. It presents, in addition to the old practices known in Yi augury, four original methods developed by myself: how to tell fortunes (1) with five coppers and one silver, (2) with a pair of dice, (3) with twenty-four cards, and (4) with "subconscious numbers." Choose any one of them best suited for you. They are all based on the same theory of Yi augury and will give you the same reliable answer.

It is my hope that this book will be a useful guide to you in making decisions and plans in business, in developing new ideas, in forming prospects about your sales, negotiations, travelling, health, marriage, dates, money making, stock and other market investments, and in finding your way in everything else, giving you invaluable advice and answering all your questions.

For your convenience, a ready guide to your fortune appears on the front and rear end-papers of this book. After you have learned to arrive at one of the combinations that will lead you to your fortune, you will find it listed on either the front or back end-papers, along with the appropriate page number.

In my opinion, the four years following September, 1965, will be a period of change throughout the world, with such occurrences as major natural phenomena, deaths of world leaders, and a complex mixture of prosperous times and crises.

It is in an era like this that Yi augury should be fully utilized, and will prove most useful to anyone who has faith in it.

Jimmei Shimano

Table of Contents

PART I

ORIENTAL FORTUNE TELLING

Chapter One

Yi Augury and Your Changing Cycles of Luck

YOU perhaps have experienced at some juncture in your life that things simply wouldn't go as you wished them to, that every move you made turned out to be exactly the opposite of what you should have done. At such times, your luck was on the wane.

At other times, you may have seen things going exceedingly well, as if all the forces in the universe had been working together to bring you success, giving you the conviction that Fortune was smiling on you. Indeed she was, for your luck was on the rise.

How helpful it would be if you could learn where in this cycle of good and bad luck you now stood. You would then be able to prepare yourself accordingly—to emerge from a period of bad luck with minimum loss, and to maximize your gains in the next lucky period.

This is actually possible. For man, the lord of all creation, has a premonitory instinct, which is present more or less in every individual. At one time or another in your life, you must have experienced a mysterious "hunch" or foreboding of an approaching danger. That was when your premonitory instinct was at work.

Yi augury is a means of utilizing this instinct, and this book tells you how to do it.

There is an old Japanese saying that luck, patience and hard work are the three essentials of success. Persons who are too smart are apt to meet with unexpected failures just because of their smartness, whereas those who are seemingly slow but patient enough to work on like a horse are more likely to find their way to success. But over and beyond these two qualities—persistence and an aptitude for hard work—you need *luck*.

Some feel that luck tends to concentrate in a handful of people, so that there is not much luck left to go around. They complain that you can wait a thousand years without getting any of it. This is not true.

Luck comes around to all of us, rising and falling in a cycle. The period of each cycle varies from individual to individual. Some have frequent surges of good luck. Others have luck only occasionally, and for a very brief period. Nevertheless, there is a cycle of luck for everyone.

Notwithstanding individual variations, cycles of luck present some general patterns. Specifically, there are three-, seven-, nine-, eleven- and thirteen-year cycles.

Looking back on your past objectively, you will probably find periods of relatively good and relatively poor luck. Sometimes things generally went well, whereas at other times, you were out of Fortune's favor.

Everyone is subject to a cycle of luck, which is controlled by a variety of forces in the universe, including those of celestial bodies and specific moments (which, incidentally, are the basis of horoscopy and the augurial theory about the effect of your age on your luck in a specific year). In other words, you are being carried by the stream of your destiny.

Many people who complain that they have always been unlucky may have overlooked periods of good luck when they did come, not knowing that their luck was on the rise.

Take, for example, the game of poker, in which you often become aware of your cycle of good and bad luck. Success in poker is ascribed seventy percent to luck and thirty percent to the brain, and this predominance of luck is what makes poker a thrilling game of chance. After some training, any poker player with an average brain will be as good as most. A good player is daring when he feels he is lucky, and conservative when he realizes that his luck has taken a turn downward. He thus minimizes his loss and prepares for his next chance, which is bound to come sooner or later. This ability to "wait," knowing when to give up and when to start again, is the most important quality in a successful poker player. Whether in a game or in gambling, the hardest enemy you have to fight is yourself. Indecision, mental instability, impatience—all these must be overcome by sheer will power, and whether you can do that determines your success or failure. A wise gambler always studies his opponent objectively with a cool head, and he can wait with amazing patience. Always being on the offensive does not bring you success. You have to be agressive at lucky times and patient when you are unlucky if you want to be successful in anything—gambling or business.

Yi augury, using *hakke,* or eight basic combinations of positive and negative elements, which are common concepts in all ancient Oriental philosophy, allows you to have a glimpse of your own cycle of luck, enabling you to capitalize on your luck when it comes, and warning you when it is declining. It tells you when to stop

being aggressive and how long you should wait before luck comes to you again.

What is Yi Augury?

To understand why Yi augury is a reliable means of looking into the future, let us consider its philosophical background in historical perspective.

Its origin may be traced back to *chou-yi,* a form of augury that evolved about three thousand years ago in China under the Chou dynasty. In those days two methods were in use to divine the future. In one, called *pu,* tortoise shells and animal bones were burnt and fortunes were told from the cracks they bore. In the other, called

shih, grass (*medoki*) stems were counted. Under the dynasties following Chou, court augurs and private fortunetellers used both methods in combination. At first, *pu,* relying on burnt cracks, was more authentic; but in time *shih* with its numerical intricacies became more popular.

In the days of the Han dynasty and thereafter, the Chinese character for *yi* was understood to mean "changeability" and "ease." Another theory, noting that Yi augury conceived everything in the universe as a combination of two basic elements, positive and negative, claimed that the character *yi* was made by

combining the simpler characters for "sun" and "moon,"

standing for positive and negative, respectively. Still another theory maintained that it was a hieroglyph representing the lizard.

Today, Yi augury, as developed and handed down by the ancient Chinese sages, combines the positive and negative into eight major combinations called *hakke*. These combinations of heaven, earth, fire, water, mountain, lake, thunder and wind are further subdivided into the sixty-four minor combinations that appear on the end papers of this volume. Each of the sixty-four minor combinations contains six index variations for a total of 384 combinations. When the ancients broke these down they eventually came up with 11,520 elements representing all things in the universe.

In Chapter Two, four modern methods for arriving at the correct combination which spells out your current and future cycles of luck, are discussed. But no matter if the method used is ancient or modern, all have one common element—all are associated with a faith in mystic numbers.

To represent all 11,520 variations of fate by the use of only sixty-four combinations of elements, ancient fortunetellers gradually came to treat them as symbols. To these was further added the Confucian idea of the "Ten Wings" to complete the present system of Yi augury.

Legend has it that the eight combinations of elements, *hakke*, were developed by Fu Hsi, the index notes by Wen Wang, and the Ten Wings by Confucius. From Confucius, the system was handed down to Shang Chu, and eventually to Tien Ho, who lived in the days of the Han dynasty. The Book of Changes survived the notorious "burning of books" by the First Emperor of Chin for the reason that it pointed to the right course of action. In the Han period it became increasingly popular until Master Augurs came to hold official positions in the courts of the Emperor Hsuan and the Emperor Yuan in the first century B.C.

Chapter Two

Four Modern Methods

Yı augury may be practiced by various methods, including the four shown below. Adopt any one of them you like best, and whenever you have a question or doubt about any one, consult this book to see what you should do and when.

(1) **Five coppers and one silver**

Old coins have been used as a means of Yi augury in China since ancient times. The augur takes one or six old coins, and assumes that one face of each coin represents the positive element and the other face, the negative. Concentrating on the question he has in mind, he drops the coin or coins on a diagram showing the directions and other symbols. He thus obtains a combination of six elements (one of the sixty-four shown on the end papers and detailed in Part II), and also an index variation (one of the 384). These tell him how Fortune's wheel is turning, and what should be done and when for best results.

A modernized version of this method, invented by the author, employs five coppers and one silver. Hold these coins between your two palms, concentrate on the question you have in mind, and hold your breath. Soon, when your mind has been freed from all worldly considerations, shake the coins in your palms to mix them well, then quietly open your palms and lay the coins on the table one by one, *from bottom to top*. (In this book, the elements in each combination are arranged horizontally, the extreme right representing the bottom.)

In old Yi augury, the positive symbol is — and the negative, --. In this book, these are replaced by ○ and ●, respectively. (If coins are used, the face showing the year is taken as positive and the other side, negative.)

○	●	○	○	●	●
Positive	Negative	Positive	Positive	Negative	Negative

Now, suppose you have obtained this combination: ○●○○●●. Referring to the list of minor combinations *(Front End-paper)*, you will see that it is Ka-Zan-Ryo (No. 23. p. 90). Also note the position of the silver coin in this combination. If it is in the fourth place from the bottom (right), "4" is your index number, and your index variation is the fourth of those listed in the No. 23 section (p. 90), or Gon-I-Zan (No. 55. p. 148) This represents the next phase of your future.

The index number, varying from "1" to "6", tells you (1) where in or around the indicated phase of your cycle of fortunes you now stand, and (2) what will come after that phase. Moreover, it is understood that "5" stands for the climax of the indicated situation. Since your index number is "4" in the present case, you may assume that you are very near the indicated phase of your fortune cycle. If the number is "1" or "2," what the combination tells you is still a fairly distant possibility; if it is "6", you are nearly past the situation. The index number "4" also suggests four days, four weeks, four months, etc. If you are thinking of a period of one year, "1" through "6" may be interpreted to mean two, four, six, eight, ten, and twelve months, respectively.

With a little experience, you will be able to consider a combination with respect to its two halves of three elements each, and judge whatever you have in mind from the implications of these two major combinations.

The combination you have obtained and its index variation may be considered to represent your immediate future and more distant future, the former being potentially capable of turning into the latter, and you may assume that your present state is influenced seventy percent by the former and thirty percent by the latter.

If the combination spells good luck while the index variation foretells relatively poor luck, the chances are that you will be lucky for the moment but may meet with dangers later on. Similarly, if the combination is unfavorable and the index variation favorable, you may be sure that, despite your present difficulties, you will turn lucky at some future time.

Whatever combination you get, the "answers" it gives you have much to do with the major combinations (Heaven, Earth, Thunder, Wind, Water, Fire, Mountain, Lake—see p. 43), whose implications may be learned gradually and usefully applied to specific situations as you become familiar with the practices of Yi augury.

(2) Two dice

Any pair of bone dice commonly available will do.

But since they are vital means of learning your future, they had better be used exclusively for the purpose. Preferably, one should be white (positive) and the other black (negative), though this is not an essential requirement. If you have not two dice, one will suffice. (Some scholars claim that the mysterious nature of dice derives from Yi augury.)

Procedure: Hold the two dice in your hand, concentrate on the question you have in mind, and throw them on the table. Add the two numbers shown. If the total is an even number, call it negative ●; if an odd number, positive (○). Cast the dice six times to obtain a combination of six elements, and record them *from bottom to top* (from right to left in this book).

If you have only one die, *add* 1 to the number obtained in each case. This also is an old practice (called *tai-kyoku*) in Yi augury. If the die shows 3, add 1 and obtain 4, which is negative. If the die gives you 6, add 1 and obtain 7, which is positive.

EXAMPLES:

With two dice

(Ten-Ka-Do-Jin, No. 3. p. 53)

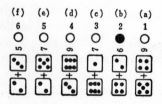

With one die

(Ten-Ka-Do-Jin, No. 3. p. 53)

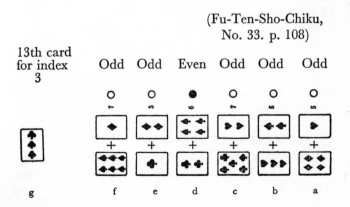

Finally, take one die to find the index number. If the die shows "4", that is your index number.

For the interpretation of the combination and the index variation, refer to the section for "Five coppers and one silver" (p. 19).

(3) Twenty-four cards

Also invented by the author, this method uses twenty-four playing cards, from ace to six of each color, selected from a deck.

(Fu-Ten-Sho-Chiku, No. 33. p. 108)

As with dice, concentrate on the question you have in mind while shuffling the twenty-four cards well. Take one card from the top and another from the bottom of the pack to make a pair. Repeat this six times and lay the six pairs in the order drawn on the table, from right to left. Finally, take the index card (thirteenth card) from the top of the pack if you are a man, and from the bottom if you are a woman. The number it shows is your index number. Also, the color of the card has various implications that may be taken into account when you interpret the meaning of your combination. Namely,

Hearts: Love, femininity, spiritual contentment, rising hope;

Diamonds: Masculinity, affection, money, material satisfaction;

Clubs: Sympathy, happiness, assistance, health;

Spades: Obstruction.

Suppose you have obtained the arrangement of cards illustrated above. From the list of Yi combinations listed on the endpapers, you will see that it is Fu-Ten-Sho-Chiku (No. 33). Since "3" is your index number, this combination is potentially capable of turning into Fu-Taku-Chu-Bu (No. 34. p. 109). Moreover, the color of the index card (clubs) suggests that you may get assistance from someone. Thus, your long-cherished wish will approach realization as promised in Fu-Taku-Chu-Bu.

(4) Subconcious numbers

(If you have never had a dream, or do not dream any more, this method will not work. Use some other method.)

Earliest records of man's history attest to the importance of numbers. Ancient Chinese philosophers thought that numbers, apart from their quantitative implications, each had an unique individuality and constituted a sort of society in which each member had specific characteristics and were in specific relationships with others.

There have been "sacred numbers" since ancient times. They were associated with supernatural forces and considered to have divine attributes. Other numbers were abhorred. The old Israelites believed that 7 was holy, 12 lucky, and 6 undesirable. They esteemed 7 and 12 because 3 represented Heaven and 4, Earth; 7 is their sum, and 12, their product. It was on this belief that they divided into twelve tribes.

Among the Indians in America, 4 was esteemed as the divine number (standing for the four directions—east west, north, and south).

Sacred numbers lend mystic qualities to the events associated with them, and T. W. Danzel divides them into "objective" and "subjective" groups.

All things around us—the sun and the earth, mountains and rivers, stones and soil, grass and trees, animals and man, air and rain—are made up of countless particles, known as atoms in modern science, and the properties of an atom depends on the number of electrons circling its nucleus. One more electron or less makes the difference between nitrogen and carbon. This is another example of the mystery of numbers.

In Yi augury, numbers reveal what certain things are and how they change.

Have you ever felt particular attraction to a certain

number? For instance, you may have had much to do with the number "3" since your childhood; or you may be particularly lucky with a certain number in gambling; or you may be generally unlucky on days related to the number "9." Such numbers may be based on the day and time of your birth or on your name. In any case, it is undeniable that there *are* such mystic numbers, as is often evidenced by statistical research.

A particular number may accompany you as long as you live, or it may change suddenly at a turning point of your life.

In this book, such numbers are called "subconscious numbers," for they are always present in your subconscious.

Yi augury uses various aids—divining blocks, bamboo sticks, dice, playing cards, the abacus, etc.—all for the purpose of casting light on the numbers that determine your fortune. The "subconscious-number" method of divination reveals such numbers by the use of man's premonitory instinct and inspiration. Numbers can symbolize various things in the universe more freely than words. Indeed, each number has intrinsic predictive implications.

Apart from subconscious numbers, "conscious numbers" you are clearly aware of may be used in combination with the numbers representing the date of your birth to determine, say, whether you will make a nice couple with another person with different mystic numbers and a different date of birth.

Basic "Subconscious Numbers"

Any of the following basic numbers may be your

favorite number. Shown below are some of their implications:

日 **1** 勿

Singular and positive, it promises you ascendancy over other people. You are independent, self-reliant, brave, daring, heroic, generous, and willing to help others. But you are too strongly principled and uncompromising. This last quality, when carried too far, sometimes puts you in helpless isolation. You are cut out for leadership in your group, class, or country. But you tend to oppose anyone threatening to surpass you. Hence you are often dogmatic. In an unfavorable environment, you may become the leader of disreputable citizens.

The number suggests material ore. Though highly valuable potentially, it is useless as it is. Refining will turn it into a precious metal. Similarly, moral training will make you a most useful member of society. Rather coarse in appearance, you need a more refined mental attitude and a softer way of talking.

If you are a woman, you are rather masculine and aggressive. You will make a good career woman. In the house, you tend to be a domineering wife.

The general pattern of your fortune is eventful until you reach middle age, and more benevolent in later years.

White is your favorite color. You are active and urban.

Illnesses affecting your chest and up should be feared. Be careful of your blood pressure, left lung, and skin.

The season symbolized by the number is October to November, which will mark the turning point, whether favorable or unfavorable, in the cycle of your changing luck.

日 **2** 勿

It is the extreme negative number and suggests the womb, from which life springs.

Generally, you are resourceful, ingenious, flexible, and sociable, but tend to commit serious slips of the tongue. Soft outside but a little cold inside, you often come up with clever ideas but lack decision to carry them out, letting opportunities slip away.

You are meticulous about small matters and often overlook important things. In some cases you are negligent, showing much enthusiasm on a proposition at first but giving it up easily as soon as it becomes a little complicated. Slight discontent underlies your happiness. If you reflect on these shortcomings as well as on your tendency to negativism and caprice, you will be a very useful member of society.

Love affairs will sometimes bring you danger. If you are a woman, you are or will make a good, sweet housewife. But you vulnerable to temptations.

As for the general pattern of your fortune, your status will become stable after you are forty-five, and anything you earn thereafter will stay with you for the rest of your life.

White or gold is the color for you. You are cut out for jobs related to the mouth—newspaperman, announcer, actress (if you are a woman), etc.

Illnesses you are likely to contract include nervous breakdown, and mouth, tooth, and throat diseases.

Autumn will mark the turning point in your fortune cycle.

日 3 勿

Positive and negative are in good harmony in this number.

You are intelligent, enterprising, happy and merry on the surface but melancholic inside, confident, emotional, easily excited and easily cooled. Fond of showiness, you start a thing with a great deal of enthusiasm and make rapid progress, but begin to lose eagerness when you are about half way through. You need constant excitement to achieve your goal.

You tend to look at things from an original viewpoint of your own, and sometimes have unusual success on that account. At other times, when circumstances are not favorable, you may fail to be accepted by others. You are always interested in novelties, and in fact your range of interest is a little too extensive. You feel gloomy at home and become happier as soon as you go out. Hence you are inclined to spend more time out of home. Living away from your parents, you are liable to succumb to sexual temptations.

As your first marriage is likely to be a failure, you are advised to marry late rather than early in your life.

As your good luck will reach its climax when you are at middle age, try to establish yourself permanently around that time.

Red or violet is the color for you.

You are cut out for a novelist, actor, teacher, or judge.

Illnesses you are likely to contract include heart and eye diseases.

Summer will mark the height of your activity.

日 4 勿

You are progressive, fond of trying new things and expanding, full of vitality and active, but a little lacking in solidity. Carelessness and frivolity may lead you to failure.

Though aggressive on the surface, you have a soft heart. Short tempered and easily excited, you often lose friends, which is a minus factor in the making of your fortune. You are likely to make a name in society or in your group while still young, but your material well being will be short of what you would expect from your ostensible status.

You give up things with philosophical calm, but you need more fight and persistence. Try to save whenever you can so that you will be able to grab opportunities for successes when they come. With your potentialities for growth, you will be able to achieve financial success sooner than most other people.

Blue or green is the color for you.

You are cut out for an announcer, radio actor, writer, singer, or any other job related to sound.

Illnesses you are likely to contract include neuralgia, asthma, bruised limbs, hysteria, and liver diseases.

Spring is your season.

日 5 勿

You are gentle, amiable, sociable, a little uneven-tempered and hence, seemingly whimsical. Well balanced and refined in appearance, you you have a gift for organization, and are considered trustworthy and reliable. You are sensitive and emotional.

Like the wind of spring, you are leisurely and care-free, and tend to be diverted from your main course. Perhaps you are capricious. From your younger days on, you tend to leave your home and move from one place to another.

As for the general pattern of your fortune, you mature early, win public recognition while you are still young, and get along with the help of older people Trust in this favorable tendency and don't be too agressive. If you are too harsh, people will eventually drop you. You will do well on your job but your income will be less than you would expect from your status.

Blue, green, or white is the color for you.

You are cut out for an architect, tourist guide, or any other job in the communication or transportation field.

Illnesses you are likely to contract include diseases affecting your respiratory organs, gullet, nerves, and intestines, although you are fairly resistant to disease.

Your luck will start increasing around April and May.

日 6 勿

The prestige of your ancestors and parents has given

you a carefree childhood. But after coming of age you will not find it easy to make a living, although you will enjoy established security in your latter years. If you don't work hard enough, however, you may end your life with no accomplishments to speak of. You are mild on the surface but have a stout heart. You may be meticulous and sensitive or apathetic and inflexible. In any case you are aggressive. You know much of the world and are introversive. Sometimes it is hard to see what you are really thinking.

You seem to be intent on economizing on this and that, but on some things you are unwittingly wasteful, though your general luck with money will always help you tide over a crisis. You will not make money on speculation, however.

Black is the color for you.

You are cut out for a philosopher, priest, laundryman, or fish monger.

Illnesses you are likely to contract include kidney, spine, uterus, and venereal diseases.

Winter is your season.

日 フ 勿

You seem stubborn and self-assertive on the surface but are considerate and warm in your heart. You have lofty ideals, but in some cases you may be asking too much.

Even if you are not the first-born, you have enough caliber to become the head of your family or some other family. You are interested in starting on a modest scale and achieving big success eventually. If you are a conservative type, you will concentrate on saving; if a showy type, you will seek all or nothing on speculative propositions. You are daring and circumspect at the same time, broad-minded and understanding. Without sufficient education, however, you may become unreasonably stubborn, making snap decisions which will be capricious rather than logical, and ruin yourself on that account. Self-reflection, sympathy for others, and careful thinking are what you need most. Your tendency to move frequently from one residence to another or to switch from one job to another will not be good for you.

The general pattern of your fortune suggests that you will have more luck toward the end of your life. While you are young or middle-aged, you will have many ordeals.

Yellow or brown is the color for you.

You are cut out for a contractor or hotel proprietor.

Illnesses you are likely to contract include nose, appendix, waist, and joint troubles.

Early spring is your season.

日 8 勿

You are either very brave or insensitive. In any case, you are patient, persistent, stubborn, self-willed, and a little venturesome. You have a talent for raking in money and property, but you may be considered greedy if you go too far.

You will be in an important position in your group. If you are a woman, you will make a successful career woman but may not be very happy at home. Being highly capable, you often think others' progress too slow, and are eager to take over and do everything in your own way, for which you may be called arbitrary or obtrusive. Generally, however, you are broad-minded enough to accept a necessity whether you like it or not. This quality will make you increasingly popular and help you get along. Both the general pattern of your fortune and your inborn nature tend to lead you to extremes, which means that you will be extremely successful if you are lucky and extremely unsuccessful if you are unlucky.

Whether you are a man or woman, you are apt to lose opportunities on account of sex problems. Remember that sex can cause your downfall. In your latter years, you will be successful and have many nice children.

Yellow is the color for you.

You are cut out for an entertainer, financier, or commentator.

Illnesses you are likely to contract include intestinal troubles, hemorrhoids, stomach ailments, uterus and other cancers, and food poisoning.

The middle of each of the four seasons will mark a turning point in your fortune cycle.

日 9 勿

You are steady and reliable, but sometimes you are insensibly honest. Stubborn, eccentric, and persistent, you are nevertheless vulnerable to temptations, whether you are a man or a woman. On the other hand, you are outwardly gentle, industrious, and patient. These qualities will help you go a long way. Whatever you do, you are advised to proceed on a long-range plan and with the guidance of seniors.

In your younger days you have not much luck. You will stay low for a fairly long time, but this period will be your vital stepping-stone for future success. After forty-five you will be established in security, and your latter years will be peaceful and happy.

Yellow is the color for you.

You are cut out for a porcelain or curio shop proprietor, building or painting contractor, or public servant.

Illnesses you are likely to contract include troubles affecting your abdomen or right hand, stomach cancer, jaundice, insomnia, and skin diseases.

The vital season for you is July to August.

日 〇 勿

If you are particularly attracted to this number, you are in an unbalanced mental state. It stands for void. You may be sensitive and talented as an artist, but if you do not take good care of yourself, you may die young, and then everything will be null and void.

How to Tell Fortunes From Subconscious Numbers

In addition to these basic numbers, you may have two-figure and three-figure numbers. Since the key number in Yi augury is "8" (standing for the eight major combinations of elements), any such number should be divided by 8. If the remainder is 0, your subconscious number is 8. In other cases, the remainder represents your subconscious number. For instance, if you have

"1963" in mind, divide it by 8. The quotient is 245 and the remainder is 3. Therefore, "3" is your subconscious number.

This procedure is simple, but don't think light of it since it is not a game. Remember that you are seeking serious advice. First, concentrate on the question you have in mind. If it is hard for you to concentrate, hold your breath about one minute until you feel blank in the head. From your subconscious, a number will emerge. Take is down on a piece of paper. Repeat this six times, and record the six numbers from bottom to top in the order of their emergence. It does not matter how many figures are in each number. The six numbers may include the year you were born, the number of the contract you have just obtained, or the plate number of your car. Whatever they are, they are the keys to your subconscious numbers, which in turn will provide the right answers to your questions.

Now, look at the first digit of each number. If it is an odd number, it stands for the positive element; if an even number, the negative. The time at which you are doing all this (such as 8 a.m. or 4 p.m.) will give you the index number, which may be used to determine your index variation.

Suppose you have obtained this series of numbers: 11, 18, 27, 809, 7, 351. They are positive, negative, positive, positive, positive, positive. The combination (O●OOOO) is Ka-Ten-Tai-Yu (No. 17 p. 79). And suppose the time is 1600 hours. Since each combination has six index variations, divide 16 by 6, and take the remainder as your index number. In this case it is 4. Your index variation, therefore, is San-Ten-Tai-Chiku

(No. 49 p. 136. ○●●○○○), the fourth element from the bottom reversed from positive to negative. Similarly, if the time is 8 a.m., your index number is 2; and if the remainder is 0, you take 6 as your index number.

Referring this combination and index variation to the Book of Changes, and taking your "subconscious number" into consideration, you can tell your fortune with accuracy. This procedure involves some telepathy and inspiration, but anyone can practice it. With a little experience, you will soon be able to tell others' fortunes as well as yours.

Chapter Three

Six Prohibitions

W HENEVER you want to tell your fortune, the
following six basic prohibitions in Yi augury
must be strictly observed:
1. Don't ask the same question more than once at a
time. Allow at least a day, or preferably three days,
before you try again; and put the question in a little
different way.

Some people ask the same question again and again
until they get a favorable answer. But the Book of
Changes warns you: "The first answer is reliable; the
second and third answers are disturbed, and disturbed
answers tell you nothing."

The second answer is only complementary to the first,
and the latter remains valid no matter how many times
you try. So, try just once.
2. Don't try to tell your fortune generally without a
specific question in mind.

Since the main purpose of Yi augury is to tell you how
Fortune's wheel is turning for you, it is pointless to ask
whether you will be lucky or unlucky without a specific
period in mind. For instance, your question should be,
"Will I be lucky this month?" or, "Will my plan succeed
within six months from now?"

If you have two marriage proposals, don't ask, "Which
should I take?" Make your question more specific, i.e.,

Am I right in thinking that this proposal is better than the other?" If you get the negative answer, then you should ask a separate question about the other proposal. If the answer is still negative, you should realize that it is still premature for you to marry. You should wait until the signal turns green.

3. Don't evaluate your fortune subjectively. Look at yourself from the viewpoint of an impartial observer, detached and disinterested. Unless your mind is free of all considerations of self-interest, the answer you get will be disturbed, or you are likely to interpret it in a way favorable to you.

4. Don't look at other answers than the one to your specific question. Of course, you may refer to the statements under the "Book of Changes" and "Comments" headings, and the general descriptions of the Eight Major Combinations, which contain useful suggestions for you.

But when you are seeking an answer on how you will be doing as a salesman, don't look at the answer about your marrying opportunities. Irrelevant answers will tell you nothing.

5. Don't ignore the warning when you have obtained one of the four worst combinations in Yi augury. They are, in the order of seriousness:

Kan-I-Sui .... ●○●●○● (No. 46. p. 130)
Taku-Sui-Kon .... ●○○●○● (No. 14. p. 73)
Sui-Zan-Ken .... ●○●○●● (No. 47. p. 132)
Sui-Rai-Chun .... ●○○●●○ (No. 44. p. 126)

Any one of these tells you to stop whatever you have been doing, although your index variation may give you some relief. You should even make a U turn. Turn back and retreat. Without wasting any more time, give up your plan or whatever you are working at once for all. No matter how attractive the proposition may seem, you will be sorry if you jump at it. Never ignore the warning you have got.

6. Never seek an answer on any proposition involving (1) murder, (2) adultery, (3) robbery, or (4) falsehood. Common sense will tell you that none of these will pay.

PART II

YI COMBINATIONS, MAJOR AND MINOR

Chapter One

Major Combinations (*Hakke*)

HAKKE (or *hakka*) means the eight basic patterns that afford the sixty-four combinations of elements making up the system of yi augury. They are:

☰—Ken, or Heaven—○○○

☷—Kon, or Earth—●●●

☳—Shin, or Thunder—●●○

☴—Son, or Wind—○○●

☵—Kan, or Water—●○●

☲—Ri, or Fire—○●○

☶—Gon, or Mountain—○●●

☱—Da, or Lake—●○○

Called the "Major Combinations" *(Shosei Hakke)*, these combine with each other to form the sixty-four minor varieties.

The *hakke* combinations are symbols which express all things in the universe better than any language. With experience, you can make an advanced interpretation of a *hakke* combination through association of ideas.

(In this book, ○ is used to denote the positive element

and ●, the negative; they also represent odd and even numbers, respectively.)

The Major Combinations have the following basic meanings, which serve as guides in interpreting the sixty-four Minor Combinations:

KEN (○○○) ≡

Symbolizes "HEAVEN," "1."

INTERPRETATION: Health, completeness, vigor, firmness, metal, high structures, churches, shrines, theaters, parliaments, stock exchanges, vehicles, nice food, blood pressure, skin diseases, ice, dogs, melons, mares, gears, space, Father, men, dignitaries, seniors, old people, foreigners, police, soldiers, white, red, anything related to the head, the left lung, nails, calcium, formic acid, canned products, ice cream.

DIRECTION: Northwest

SEASON: October-November

TIME: 9 p.m.-11 p.m.

MARKET TREND: Upward, bullish

KON (●●●) ☷

Symbolizes "Earth," "8."

INTERPRETATION: Tenderness, obedience, stoutness, void, suspicion, Mother, fellow workers, relatives, Wife, subordinates, clothing, food and housing, home, going down, hesitation, dust color, black, the belly, pregnancy, broken things, old things, wicked people, waste land, cripples, failures, the intestines, constipation, loose bowels, miscarriage, piles, poisonous plants.

DIRECTION: Southwest

SEASON: August-October

TIME: 2 p.m.-5 p.m.

MARKET TREND: Sluggish, bearish, near the bottom.

SHIN (●●○) ☰

Symbolizes "THUNDER," "4."

INTERPRETATION: Vibration, turning, going well, budding, impatience, going too far, anything related to sound, electricity, vegetables and sea weed, flirtation, quickness, simplicity, the first son, the leader, forests, blue, going up, anything related to the limbs, spring, power plants, announcer, pianos, records, pistols, the liver, the tongue, the throat, asthma, hysteria, rheumatism, deafness.

DIRECTION: East

SEASON: February-April

TIME: Early morning

MARKET TREND: Upward, with chain-reaction buying.

SON (○○●) ☰

Symbolizes "WIND," "5."

INTERPRETATION: Indecision, length, things coming and going, calling out, following, optimism, mildness, home, learning, small things, plants, love affairs, wife, the first daughter, business, telephones, flying, carpenters, thighs, marriage, roads, thin lines, engineers, travelers, brokers, the intestines, the left hand, the hair, the nerves, the gullet, dead grass.

DIRECTION: Southeast

SEASON: April-June

TIME: 6 a.m.-9 a.m.

MARKET TREND: Unchanged, bearish.

KAN (●○●) ☵

Symbolizes "WATER," "6."

INTERPRETATION: Caving in, falling, anxiety, being cheated, difficulty, darkness, drinks, wife, cold things, middle-aged men, a middle (neither first nor last) son, vehicles, slander, black, red, blood, anything related to the ear, listening, broadcasting, intercourse, hospitals, gas stations, beaches, rivers, the native place, typewriters, cocktails, the dead, nuns, sculptors, people with birth-marks or moles, blindness, the kidneys, the uterus, the spine, the genitals.

DIRECTION: North

SEASON: Winter, November-January

TIME: Midnight

MARKET TREND: Further down.

RI (○●○) ☲

Symbolizes "FIRE," "3."

INTERPRETATION: Passion, beautiful women, a middle (neither first nor last) daughter, beautiful things, intelligence, anything related to fire or light, letters, motion pictures and television, department stores, accessories, ovens, stock-certificates, bills, books, maps, national flags, shrines, schools, beauty parlors, government offices, justices, pregnant women, bald-headed men, novelists, actors and actresses, athletes, wine, shells, horse races, dandelions, eyes, records, writing, red and violet, anything related to the eye, the heart, the brains, the breasts.

DIRECTION: South

SEASON: Summer, July-September

TIME: Noon

MARKET TREND: Temporarily upward.

GON (○●●) ☰☰

Symbolizes "MOUNTAIN," "7."

INTERPRETATION: Stopping, being serious and stubborn, motionlessness, warehouses, stations, minor independence, studying, admission to a school, hands, joints, rocks, little boys, youth, yellow or dust-colored things, family privileges, anything related to the hands, fat people, brokers, heirs, meat dishes, the nose, the belly, muscles.

DIRECTION: Northeast

SEASON: January-March

TIME: 1 a.m.-3 a.m.

MARKET TREND: Upward with a limit.

DA (●○○) ☰☰

Symbolizes "LAKE," "2."

INTERPRETATION: Peace, little things, kisses, happy developments, anything related to the mouth, announcers, actresses, restaurants, bars, mistresses, shipyards, musical instruments, headless things, financing, lawyers, brokers, evening primroses, water plants, damp places, incompleteness, weakness, good friends, maidens, white or gold, joy of generation, wedding, sharp edges, the right lung, nervous breakdown, landslides.

DIRECTION: West

SEASON: Autumn, September-November

TIME: 8 p.m.-10 p.m.

MARKET TREND: Inactive and low, staying at the bottom.

In interpreting a note in the Book of Changes, the symbolic meaning of a Major Combination may be stretched freely with the help of experience, associations and common sense.

Chapter Two

Minor Combinations . . . Yi Fortunes

"Heaven" ○○○ Combinations

1. Ken-I-Ten ○○○ ○○○
   Extreme Happiness is Close
   to Sorrow.

BOOK OF CHANGES: A dragon
   ascending to Heaven is your
   symbol. You are extremely lucky. But remember, a
   full moon is bound to wane.
   Don't count too much on
   your luck.

COMMENTS: This combination is all positive, very virile
and manly. After long staying underground, the dragon is now rising energetically to reach Heaven. Your
luck is tremendous. In seasonal terms, it symbolizes
April.

   If you get this combination but are not doing well
right now, you may be sure that you have a bright
future before you, with all past worries and sufferings
quickly diminishing. You are right at the turning
point. Don't be impatient, for soon everything will
start going well.

   Being the first combination listed, it is taken as sup-
reme and paramount, symbolic of a beginning, a good

beginning for people in noble or high status and for diligent workers. But it is "too good" for lazy, insincere, or conceited persons. They may be faring well at the present moment, but their luck may expire quickly and start declining sharply like a stock that has been too high. After reaching the summit, the only way you can go is downward. Beware of a complete reversal of your luck.

If you are a woman, you are rather masculine, spirited and aggressive—good qualities in a businesswoman— but a little too argumentative and conscious of your intelligence. You may not be a good housewife, but you have an aptitude for money-making. You are well-to-do. But always try to save. You tend to spend as much as you earn. You may have a major change in six months.

GENERAL: Everything begins now. It is a good time to start a business or a project. You will make a name first, and get material gains later.

WISHES: Reasonable wishes will come true. Talk to a superior for best results. You will have success in getting a job or in an examination.

MARRIAGE: Good for a woman, but generally not very favorable for a man unless he is marrying into the woman's family. She tends to be aggressive in everything.

BIRTH: You will have a son.

HEALTH: Beware of brain and nerve diseases. You are under a mental stress.

NEGOTIATIONS, DISPUTES: Get an intermediary and give him a free hand.

TEN-TAKU-RI

TRAVELING: Generally favorable. But don't be reckless. You might get hurt.

MISSING PROPERTY: Look southwest.

AWAITED PERSONS: Coming, though late.

MONEY: Things look so grand that you tend to go too far. You might lose money that way. Be careful.

MARKET: It will rise, reach a peak, then start down.

INDEX VARIATIONS:*

		6 5 4 3 2 1*
1st place:	Ten-Pu-Ko	○○○○○●
2nd place:	Ten-Ka-Do-Jin	○○○○●○ (2*)
3rd place:	Ten-Taku-Ri	○○○●○○ (3*)
4th place:	Fu-Ten-Sho-Chiku	○○●○○○ (4*)
5th place:	Ka-Ten-Tai-Yu	○●○○○○ (5*)
6th place:	Taku-Ten-Kai	●○○○○○ (6*)

*Note: You will see from these variations that if the index is 1, the last element in the combination becomes negative; if it is 2, the second element from the last; etc. In any case, the variation you get represents what will happen to you in a more distant future.

2. Ten-Taku-Ri ○○○ ●○○ Select a Good Partner in a Crisis.

BOOK OF CHANGES: You are running the risk of stepping on a tiger's tail. But proceed in good form, and you will succeed.

COMMENTS: *Ri* means courtesy. Be courteous, pay respect to your superiors and do everything in your limited power.

With modesty, proceed behind other people if you want to succeed. But there is always a risk. A venture started in a half-hearted manner will bring you considerable worries later on.

The combination also symbolizes female nudity with a tendency to nymphomania. Beware of men!

Fatalists talk about your destiny, which means the lot you were born with. For instance, if three office girls try to tell their own fortunes on the same proposition and get the same Yi combination (which almost never happens in practice), it does not follow that they will follow similar courses in life. Even if the combination promises "good luck", the first girl may have, say, 80 percent of the potential luck; the second girl, 70 percent; and the third girl, 50 percent. The percentage will be limited by your capacity for luck. A pint bottle cannot hold more than a pint of milk. Therefore, know your limitations, and be modest.

GENERAL: A surprise will be followed by a joy. Be careful not to lose courtesy in dealing with seniors and superiors.

WISHES: Wishes out of proportion to your status will not be granted.

MARRIAGE: After a tentative hitch, you will hear the wedding bells. A little anxiety remains, however.

BIRTH: You will have a daughter in a safe delivery.

HEALTH: You will be generally fine, but if you contract a disease, it will last. Beware of respiratory and venereal diseases.

TEN-KA-DO-JIN

NEGOTIATIONS, DISPUTES: Courtesy is most important. Private negotiations concerning future consequences are preferable to legal action.

TRAVELING: There will be a surprise. Don't flirt.

MISSING PROPERTY: Ask a woman, though you have a slim chance of finding it.

AWAITED PERSONS: You will hear from him (her) soon.

MONEY: The situation looks promising, but it will not amount to much. If you are dazzled by a prospect of immediate gains and lose courtesy, you will suffer a heavy loss.

MARKET: After a lull, there will be an unfavorable turn. Don't venture, or you will smart from it.

INDEX VARIATIONS:

1st place:	Ten-Sui-Sho	○○○●○●
2nd place:	Ten-Rai-Bu-Mo	○○○●●○
3rd place:	Ken-I-Ten	○○○○○○
4th place:	Fu-Taku-Chu-Bu	○○●●○○
5th place:	Ka-Taku-Kei	○●○●○○
6th place:	Dai-I-Taku	●○○●○○

3. Ten-Ka-Do-Jin ○○○ ○●○ Agreement Will Be Reached.

BOOK OF CHANGES: Symbolic of a light emerging in darkness, this combination gives you hope of eventual success.

COMMENTS: *Do-jin* signifies friendliness. You are healthy, wise, gifted with a talent for writing, and sociable. The combination is one of hope, the kind of hope that occurs in the heart of a lone traveler who, after walking hours in darkness, has found a clear light in the distance. Now you can proceed with confidence. With past hardships and worries gone, you will receive unexpected assistance, and everything will go well. You will be favored by your superiors, and your joint undertakings with associates will go a long way.

You tend to be impatient from habit, but what you need most is persistence. However, there may be some complications in your relations with kith and kin.

If you are a woman, you tend to be unfaithful, though not to the point of flirting, creating a little gulf between you and your husband or fiance. Beware.

GENERAL: Proceeding with hope, you will have assistance from a good friend.

WISHES: With the assistance of a superior or an old woman, your wish will come true sooner. Don't proceed alone. You need someone to help you.

MARRIAGE: You will succeed if you are marrying for the second time or have proper arrangements worked out directly with your prospective spouse, though you may still be interested in someone else.

BIRTH: The delivery will be safe.

HEALTH: You are under a little stress. Take care of yourself. Beware of fevers and epidemics.

NEGOTIATIONS, DISPUTES: You can achieve a settlement by showing modesty. Conciliation with the help of a person of high status is advisable.

TRAVELING: You will be lucky on a trip with a companion, but traveling with a member of the opposite sex might entail unfavorable consequences.

MISSING PROPERTY: It will be found if you look for it at once.

AWAITED PERSONS: Coming without fail.

MONEY: You will have your share. But don't seek both

TEN-RAI-BU-MO

money and carnal pleasures at the same time. You will lose a good friend that way.

INDEX VARIATIONS:

1st place:	Ten-Zan-Ton	......○○○○●●
2nd place:	Ken-I-Ten	........○○○○○○
3rd place:	Ten-Rai-Bu-Mo	....○○○●●○
4th place:	Fu-Ka-Ka-Jin	......○○●○●○
5th place:	Ri-I-Ka	...........○●○○●○
6th place:	Taku-Ka-Kaku	......●○○○●○

4. Ten-Rai-Bu-Mo

○○○ ●●○ Leave it to Heaven.

BOOK OF CHANGES: Thunder is rolling in summer and everything is swaying, unsettled. Don't take action in haste.

COMMENTS: You may be anxious about many things at the moment, but the time is not ripe for you to take any action. Relax and wait. Leave everything to Heaven, and don't over-reach yourself. Since your luck is not as yet high enough, let things go without interfering. If you count on your brain and make a move, you are bound to fail. So, stop being impatient and mark time. Things will turn in your favor pretty soon as luck comes back to you.

If you are expecting to marry, let things take their own course, and don't count too much on marrying. If you have a lover, there will be some complication.

GENERAL: Everything depends on chance. You are in an unstable situation.

TEN-PU-KO

WISHES: It will not be granted until the time comes.

MARRIAGE: You will find it hard to marry him (her), with disagreements cropping up. However, you will have success if you are marrying for the second time.

BIRTH: A boy will be delivered safe and sound.

HEALTH: You will be sleepless, and might fall ill suddenly. Be careful.

NEGOTIATIONS, DISPUTES: You are generally at a disadvantage.

TRAVELING: You will be lucky if you follow others' advice. But business trips are not commendable.

MISSING PROPERTY: It will not be found. Someone has misappropriated it.

AWAITED PERSONS OR MESSAGES: Not coming due to a mistake on the way.

MONEY: You will be disappointed.

MARKET: Generally unchanged, with minor ups and downs. Buying as others do will bring you immediate gains, but a heavy loss will be in store for you if you go too far.

INDEX VARIATIONS:

1st place:	Ten-Chi-Hi	........○○○●●●
2nd place:	Ten-Taku-Ri	........○○○●○○
3rd place:	Ten-Ka-Do-Jin	....○○○○●○
4th place:	Fu-Rai-Eki	........○○●●●○
5th place:	Ka-Rai-Zei-Go	....○●○●●○
6th place:	Taku-Rai-Zui	......●○○●●○

5. Ten-Pu-Ko ○○○ ○○● Things Will Just Happen.

BOOK OF CHANGES: The fruit is ripe on the tree, ready to be picked or fall. Stay alert, or you might have an unpleasant surprise.

COMMENTS: *Ko* means an accident. By accident you may

meet an unexpected disaster. Beware of traffic accidents and frauds. If you are an office girl, you are in a position to be embarrassed by a superior's special kindness for you, and the man in your heart unfortunately has evil intentions about you. You had better not try to get married at this moment. Talk to people you can really trust. Trying to have your own way in everything will merely bring you disaster.

Generally, problems tend to crop up where they have been least expected, making seemingly simple things difficult for you. So, stay on guard, and continue to do your best.

However, this combination symbolizes a state of things quickly coming and going, and is good for gay trades. In seasonal terms, it represents May.

GENERAL: Your luck is turning down. Stay on guard.

WISHES: It will not be granted easily, with problems cropping up.

MARRIAGE: You will not be able to marry him (her) due to interference from above.

BIRTH: There may be a little trouble. Take balanced nourishment, and take good care of yourself after the confinement.

HEALTH: A slight illness may linger on. Beware of constipation.

NEGOTIATIONS, DISPUTES: You will be at a considerable disadvantage. Seek conciliation through an intermediary.

TRAVELING: You are likely to have trouble with the opposite sex. Seek no carnal pleasures away from home, or you will be in a mess.

MISSING PROPERTY: A woman is involved, and it will be found quite unexpectedly.

TEN-SUI-SHO

AWAITED PERSONS, MESSAGES: Coming if you ask.

MONEY: You need to economize now, though you will get a little money now and then.

MARKET: Tensely balanced with considerable fluctuations.

INDEX VARIATIONS:

1st place:	Ken-I-Ten	○○○○○○
2nd place:	Ten-Zan-Ton	○○○○●●
3rd place:	Ten-Sui-Sho	○○○●○●
4th place:	Son-I-Fu	○○●○○●
5th place:	Ka-Fu-Tei	○●○○○●
6th place:	Taku-Fu-Tai-Ka	●○○○○●

6. Ten-Sui-Sho ○○○ ●○● It's No Use to Argue.

BOOK OF CHANGES: *Sho* means suing. There will be a dispute.

COMMENTS: This combination symbolizes disharmony between Heaven and Man. In a company, there will be a lack of unity, or even an open rift. You are not of harmony with your superiors, and find everything going against your will. But don't be impatient, or you will fall into an adverse situation from which it will be very hard for you to emerge. Counting on your brain and forcing your way will bring you disaster due to miscalculations. But you will find a way out if you talk to a proper superior or friend and follow his advice. Bear in mind that your luck is very low at this moment, and act accordingly with modesty. You may be involved in a fraud or a suit, and cannot expect much success in marrying. If you are a woman, you may find yourself in an awkward position between two parties.

Like a willow bowing to the wind, keep your head low and try to get along with others.

GENERAL: Your luck is on the wane. Refrain from new undertakings, and wait until your luck recovers.

BIRTH: A boy will be born safe.

HEALTH: You tend to have circulatory disturbance, complaints due to exposure to cold, rheumatism, neuralgia; if you are a man, early impotence; if you are a woman, suppressed desires.

NEGOTIATIONS, DISPUTES: There will be considerable discrepancies between the two parties. In the case of a suit, you had better seek a private settlement.

TRAVELING: Generally you had better not go on any trip, unless you are going alone for pleasure.

MISSING PROPERTY: No use looking for it; someone has it.

AWAITED PERSONS, MESSAGES: Not coming due to a misunderstanding. There may be a little chance, however, if you send word with modesty.

MONEY: You are likely to be disappointed, but you will be helped by a woman or an inferior. Keep an eye on your locker or desk. Beware of thieves.

MARKET: You are likely to lose. Whether you buy or sell, the market will turn against your expectations. Don't borrow money for market investment, or you will be sued later. There are times when you should do nothing in the market. The general trend will be downward, if you insist on having an answer.

INDEX VARIATIONS:

1st place:	Ten-Taku-Ri	○○○●○○
2nd place:	Ten-Chi-Hi	○○○●●●
3rd place:	Ten-Pu-Ko	○○○○○●
4th place:	Fu-Sui-Kan	○○●●●○
5th place:	Ka-Sui-Bi-Sai	○●○●○●
6th place:	Taku-Sui-Kon	●○○●○●

TEN-ZAN-TON

7. Ten-Zan-Ton ○○○ ○●● Flying is the Best Tactic.

BOOK OF CHANGES: *Ton* means flying or retreating. The combination symbolizes a wise man retreating into the woods. You will be lucky if you turn back. If you are an entertainer or an educator, you will have much luck by going forward.

COMMENTS: You will lose by advancing and gain by retreating. Since your luck is declining, move back to reduce your battle front and consolidate your defenses. Think hard. You have a lot of problems at this time and are faced with malice from envious people and slanderers. Everything has gone wrong and is in a mess. If you stand absent-minded, moreover, you are likely to meet with an accident, possibly a truck rushing upon you.

Generally, you will be unlucky at first and then find yourself luckier with the lapse of time. If you are in difficulty or adversity now, you may assume that you will soon be out of the trouble. Perhaps you should make a positive move if you see a chance. But you might court more trouble that way unless you keep in mind the general state of things around you. Now is the time to think hard and take a resolute action. This combination is essentially a hard one spelling difficulties, but it is very lucky for people in service trades or in motion picture, theater and entertainment fields. You may expect to make a hit production.

GENERAL: Your luck is going down. But you will have much luck if you are operating in entertainment, night club, and other gay businesses.

WISHES: It will not come true due to interference.

TEN-CHI-HI

MARRIAGE: Your chances of marrying are generally low.

BIRTH: Beware of miscarriage.

HEALTH: A seemingly slight ailment will tend to linger. You are losing energy and getting weaker.

NEGOTIATIONS, DISPUTES: Your opponent will be at an advantage. There will be meddlers working against you.

TRAVELING: A pilgrimage to a shrine or church may be commendable. Ordinary trips had better be canceled.

MISSING PROPERTY: Someone has taken it away. It will not be recovered unless you take action at once.

AWAITED PERSONS, MESSAGES: Not coming for the moment due to certain problems.

MONEY: With considerable internal costs and expenses, you will not have much money as yet.

MARKET: Balanced at a high level.

INDEX VARIATIONS:

1st place:	Ten-Ka-Do-Jin	....○○○○●○
2nd place:	Ten-Pu-Ko	.......○○○○○●
3rd place:	Ten-Chi-Hi	.......○○○●●●
4th place:	Fu-Zan-Zen	.......○○●○●●
5th place:	Ka-Zan-Ryo	.......○●○○●●
6th place:	Taku-Zan-Kan	....●○○○●●

8. Ten-Chi-Hi ○○○ ●●● Man and Wife Sleep Back to Back.

BOOK OF CHANGES: There are clouds over the moon, screening its light and creating a gloom.

COMMENTS: *Hi* means negation and lack of communication. Look at the combination: the two halves are opposite to each other in polarity. In seasonal terms, it is centered around July. You are apt to be suspected by others, have a break with an old friend, or suffer from a domestic disharmony, a prospect of divorce, or other such unfortunate developments which will also affect your business. At the office, you tend to be frustrated, seeing your reasonable opinion rejected and your honest efforts ignored. But contain yourself and persevere until your luck returns. Losing your patience at this time will serve no purpose. You will merely bog down further and fall into a serious predicament. So, be patient until the gloomy mist

clears up. If the index is 2, you will have to wait two months; if it is 4, four months. After that, your current problems will turn into factors for prosperity.

In any case, it is most inadvisable to take action now. Since all doors are closed, making a move will not get you anywhere. Your lover, or even your spouse, is thinking of leaving you, not sharing your joys and sorrows any more. In the worst case, you might have a divorce.

If you are expecting to enter a school or a company, or going to employ someone or sign a contract, you had better give it up. A better opportunity will present itself soon. With respect to health, beware of brain hemorrhage due to constipation. If you are a woman, you may have skin eruptions and other such troubles.

GENERAL: Though unhappy at present, you may look forward to much happiness in the future.

WISHES: It will not come true immediately, but seventy or eighty percent of it will be realized later.

MARRIAGE: There will be some problems, but you will be able to marry if you or the other party make a few concessions.

BIRTH: There will be worries, but the baby will be born safely if you keep in touch with the doctors. The husband's cooperation is essential.

HEALTH: A brain hemorrhage or circulatory trouble may be quite dangerous. Refer to your index variation.

NEGOTIATIONS, DISPUTES: No favorable settlement will be made. With impatience, you are bound to fail.

TRAVELING: Don't go on a trip unless it is a short one.

MISSING PROPERTY: It will be hard to find.

AWAITED PERSONS, MASSAGES: Not coming due to trouble, or coming unexpectedly without warning.

MONEY: At this moment it is difficult even to borrow money. Beware of thieves. Keep an eye on your seal, deeds, etc.

MARKET: Will stay balanced despite new factors. Whichever way you act, the market will turn exactly in the opposite way.

INDEX VARIATIONS:

1st place:	Ten-Rai-Bu-Mo	....○○○●●○
2nd place:	Ten-Sui-Sho	........○○○●○○
3rd place:	Ten-Zan-Ton	......○○○○●●
4th place:	Fu-Chi-Kan	......○○●●●●
5th place:	Ka-Chi-Shin	........○●○●●●
6th place:	Taku-Chi-Sui	......●○○●●●

TAKU-TEN-KAI

"Lake" ●○○ Combinations

9. Taku-Ten-Kai ●○○ ○○○ Dangerous Isolation.

BOOK OF CHANGES: Superiors will be overpowered by inferiors in a bloodless revolution. The old state of things will change.

COMMENTS: Kai means forcing your way successfully by displacing your superiors. Your luck is high. But you are apt to stumble due to stubborness—venturing forward without prudence and falling into a serious predicament.

If your standing is high, your subordinates or subcontractors will tend to rebel against you, leaving you in isolation. Since you are a man (woman) of caliber with a resolute mind and considerable ability, you can afford to be more gentle and flexible.

When you are faring well, a sudden misfortune may befall you. A serious argument or dispute may develop over a trivial matter, and problems may occur from such things as bonds and houses. In love affairs, you tend to love someone who does not think much of you, and consequently overstrain yourself. There is disharmony between you and your spouse, and both may be thinking of divorce. A cooling period would permit both of you to reflect upon yourselves.

GENERAL: You will do very well when things are going well. But look out for a stumbling block. If you are not doing well, you should not make any move. Refer to your index variation. The present combination represents March.

WISHES: Frustration will await you halfway to the goal. Obstacles will crop up.

DA-I-TAKU

MARRIAGE: The proposition is sound, but investigate the other party thoroughly.

BIRTH: Generally safe.

HEALTH: The condition needs close watching.

NEGOTIATIONS, DISPUTES: Positive action will bring you luck. Be honest.

TRAVELING: There will be a costly surprise.

MISSING PROPERTY: It will not be recovered.

AWAITED PERSONS, MESSAGES: If you are waiting for a woman, she will come. She is trying to make up her mind now.

MONEY: A fortune will be made after a period of abject poverty. But don't count on a lottery or the like. Your past plans and ideas will bring you money.

MARKET: A spurt will be followed by a temporary fall.

INDEX VARIATIONS:

1st place:	Taku-Fu-Tai-Ka	.. ●○○○○●
2nd place:	Taku-Ka-Kaku	...... ●○○○●○
3rd place:	Da-I-Taku	.... ●○○●○○
4th place:	Sui-Ten-Ju	.... ●○●○○○
5th place:	Rai-Ten-Tai-So	.... ●●○○○○
6th place:	Ken-I-Ten	.... ○○○○○○

10. Da-I-Taku

●○○ ●○○ A Double Chance.

BOOK OF CHANGES: The combination symbolizes a new moon reflected in a lake. *Da* means happiness, which, however, is potential at present and will be realized later.

COMMENTS: Though glowing with hope, your situation is

also fraught with unsettled problems. There are worries behind an appearance of well-being.

Currently you are anxious about things which are beyond your control. Admired by some and accused by others, you are nervous and touchy. If these are coupled with carnal desires and greed for money, you will simply destroy yourself.

Da also signifies the mouth. Perhaps it would help to confide your problems to a trusted superior or friend and ask his advice. Once told, the problems will weigh less heavily on your mind. But remember, you can court trouble by talking too much. Refrain from slandering or telling on other people. It will backfire. With the help of hidden supporters, you will do increasingly well as time goes on. For the moment, try some diversion and mark time. Moreover, this combination promises you much in the pecuniary way.

You will have much luck if you are a salesman, an entertainer, a radio or television artist, a singer, a newspaperman, or anything else specially related to *da* (mouth). You are on the right track. You will be starting on a new undertaking before long.

If you are a woman, people naturally talk behind your back since you are charming and appealing. Never mind them and relax. Wait a little while and you will be exactly what you want to be. But the man you are dealing with now is not very dependable.

GENERAL: After a period of mental and physical striving, your luck will swing upward.

WISHES: It seems almost within your reach but you cannot get hold of it easily. Perhaps more explanation is needed. Try to be more persuasive.

TAKU-KA-KAKU

MARRIAGE: There will be a little difficulty. Make thorough investigations. If both of you are in the entertainment field, you may expect to marry with fair success. Especially, you will have good luck if you are marrying for the second time.

BIRTH: A girl will be born safely, though she may be a little undergrown.

HEALTH: Beware of troubles affecting the stomach, duodenum, the colon, and of food poisoning. Haven't you bad teeth?

NEGOTIATIONS, DISPUTES: A settlement will be made if you show sincerity.

TRAVELING: It will be costly, but there will be no misfortunes or accidents.

MISSING PROPERTY: It will be found if you look for it immediately. You will have a hint from a woman.

AWAITED PERSONS, MESSAGES: Word will come quick from the West. In any case, you will not wait in vain.

MONEY: Money is one thing that seems abundant but is scarce in reality. It will come to you little by little.

MARKET: The upward trend is in check. Wait for new factors.

INDEX VARIATIONS:

1st place:	Taku-Sui-Kon	●○○●○●
2nd place:	Taku-Rai-Zui	●○○●●○
3rd place:	Taku-Ten-Kai	●○○○○○
4th place:	Sui-Taku-Setsu	●○●●○○
5th place:	Rai-Taku-Ki-Mai	●●○●○○
6th place:	Ten-Taku-Ri	○○○●○○

11. Taku-Ka-Kaku ●○○ ○●○ It's Time for a Major Change.

BOOK OF CHANGES: Spelling good luck for a change, the

combination symbolizes a firefly emerging from dying grass to glow beautifully.

COMMENTS: The grass is sodden and the insect emerging from it might be expected to look ugly. But, lo, it glows with exquisite beauty! Things will turn out much better than expected, and there will be a joyous change from old to new.

At this moment you may not be in a very happy state, but with effort you will recover your luck and be admired by one and all. With increasing luck, you will be heading for success. But don't be impatient.

You will be lucky, and are already beginning to be lucky, in carrying out a reform, remodeling your house, moving to a new residence, or taking a new job. Try to take all circumstances into account and evaluate them carefully so that your change will not be one for the worse.

Whether you are a man or a woman, beware of the opposite sex. A woman might find herself with an illegitimate child. Generally, things will tend to change. An old contract may be changed, but there will be hope of future improvement.

GENERAL: Your luck is good and may be counted on. You are, as it were, coming into the limelight. In a game or battle, you will be the winner.

WISHES: After a slow start, it will quickly come true. A new plan or idea will be very fruitful.

MARRIAGE: Don't hurry. You will not be very lucky if you are marrying for the first time. Otherwise, you will have a successful marriage.

BIRTH: A boy will be born. The mother may have a little trouble after her confinement.

TAKU-RAI-ZUI

HEALTH: A lingering ailment might come to an unexpected change, possibly for the worse. Your life may be in danger. There will be a chance of survival if you change the doctor or enter a hospital and receive the best treatment from a specialist. Beware of traffic accidents involving your family.

NEGOTIATIONS, DISPUTES: Things will turn in your favor, though with a little delay.

TRAVELING: Your itinerary may be changed. You will be lucky if you are going West or South.

MISSING PROPERTY: You left it somewhere. Someone has misappropriated it.

AWAITED PERSONS, MESSAGES: Not coming due to a change of mind. There may be a little chance, however, if you are waiting for a woman.

MONEY: Even with care, you will find yourself spending too much. But you will be lucky in a game.

MARKET: There will be a turn—down from a high level or up from a low level.

INDEX VARIATIONS:

1st place:	Taku-Zan-Kan	.... ●○○○●●
2nd place:	Taku-Ten-Kai	.... ●○○○○○
3rd place:	Taku-Rai-Zui	...... ●○○●●○
4th place:	Sui-Ka-Ki-Sai	...... ●○●○●○
5th place:	Rai-Ka-Ho	.... ●●○○●○
6th place:	Ten-Ka-Do-Jin	.... ○○○○●○

12. Taku-Rai-Zui ●○○ ●●○ Float with the Stream.

BOOK OF CHANGES: *Zui* means willingness to follow. You have the luck of a follower, which may not be capital but will be reasonably good.

COMMENTS: The combination symbolizes a little girl following her big brother. You will find a good advisor, whose assistance will enable you to achieve a lot of success. But there may be others approaching you with deceptive intentions. Prudence and good judgment are essential in any case.

If you are young, you may fall into trouble due to a love affair, acting in defiance of a superior's advice and courting failure. Try to see if the party you are dealing with has evil or kind intentions. If anyone tells you to stop, stop and wait until the signal turns green. You may change your residence, or leave your home town, or quit your job, but you will be safe so long as you float with the stream.

If you are a man, you may have an attractive woman before you, and you may be tempted to switch your allegiance from your present wife or lover. The chances are that the stream will carry you in that direction, whether it will be good for you or not. If you are a product or insurance salesman, you should be contented with small orders or contracts for the moment, for they will bring you better results in the future.

This combination spells a happy marriage. The other party is anxious to marry you. As man and wife, you will get along with each other.

GENERAL: You will be busy with affairs that essentially concern other people. Your luck is moderately good, and will be better in the future.

TAKU-FU-TAI-KA

WISHES: It is likely to come true. You may ask others' help. If you want to borrow money, ask for a small sum to begin with.

MARRIAGE: The other party is eager to marry you. The wedding bells will ring very soon.

BIRTH: Safe.

HEALTH: A seemingly slight complaint could be dangerous. You had better undergo a close checkup.

NEGOTIATIONS, DISPUTES: You may be winning in name and losing in reality. The net result will be a loss.

TRAVELING: You will have no trouble.

MISSING PROPERTY: It will be found before long.

AWAITED PERSONS, MESSAGES: Coming soon.

MONEY: You tend to make much and spend much. You may borrow a little money.

MARKET: You will earn a lot—the market falling after you sell and rising after you buy. Whether rising or falling, it will be subject to considerable fluctuations.

INDEX VARIATIONS:

1st place:	Taku-Chi-Sui	●○○●●●
2nd place:	Dai-I-Taku	●○○●○○
3rd place:	Taku-Ka-Kaku	●○○○●○
4th place:	Sui-Rai-Chun	●○●●●○
5th place:	Shin-I-Rai	●●○●●○
6th place:	Ten-Rai-Bu-Mo	○○○●●○

13. Taku-Fu-Tai-Ka ●○○ ○○● Retreat a Step Before Advancing Two Steps.

BOOK OF CHANGES: On horseback you are riding into a crowded town. Don't go too fast if you want to avoid accidents.

COMMENTS: At present your luck seems capital. But since you are riding through a crowd, you should not hurry, otherwise, you might hurt pedestrians and even yourself. You have warnings in all directions. *Tai-ka* means going too far. An over-inflated balloon may seem impressive but it may burst at any time, and it is likely to shrink in time.

You are apt to be involved in a trouble which will be beyond your control. In your business, you have expanded too much and are running short of funds.

Instead of relying too much on your own judgment, listen to the opinion of others, though you may not be in a frame of mind to do so. In a love affair, you tend to go all the way to the very end, knowing you are ruining yourself that way. You have both carnal and platonic desires.

This combination warns you to retreat a step and reduce your burden, for you tend to overwork and over-exert yourself. Until all dangers pass, stay like a prudent fox calmly watching a hunter go by. Time will solve your problem, and you will soon find an open way before you. Wait a little longer with patience.

GENERAL: You will have a hard time trying to make both ends meet.

WISHES: It seems almost coming true but will never be realized.

MARRIAGE: Complications will keep you from marrying. Forcible action for marriage will cause misfortune to one of the parties.

BIRTH: The baby is overgrown and will have a hard time before it is born.

HEALTH: A man tends to be overworked and a woman, to fall ill.

TAKU-SUI-KON

NEGOTIATIONS, DISPUTES: Agreement will be hard to reach. You will be at a disadvantage if you assert yourself too much.

TRAVELING: An unexpected trouble will happen.

MISSING PROPERTY: It will not be recovered.

AWAITED PERSONS, MESSAGES: Coming, but you will not be there to receive him (her, them, it).

MONEY: You will have difficulty in raising enough money to meet immediate needs.

MARKET: It has gone out of reasonable limits. If it is at a high level, a sharp decline is forthcoming.

INDEX VARIATIONS:

1st place:	Taku-Ten-Kai	.... ●○○○○○
2nd place:	Taku-Zan-Kan	.... ●○○○●●
3rd place:	Taku-Sui-Kon	...... ●○○●○●
4th place:	Sui-Fu-Sei	.... ●○●○○●
5th place:	Rai-Fu-Ko	.... ●●○○○●
6th place:	Ten-Pu-Ko	.... ○○○○○●

14. Taku-Sui-Kon ●○○ ●○● Stay Low.

BOOK OF CHANGES: This is one of the four hardest combinations in Yi augury. *Kon* means trouble or suffering. Whatever happens, stay low. Things will improve.

COMMENTS: You are gloomily watchings things get worse minute by minute. Both physically and mentally, you are unsettled and suffering considerably, and your heart is troubled too. Possibly you are thinking of leaving home or flying by night. You may feel that you are the most unhappy creature in the world, but there are people in worse circumstances. You are somewhere between the luckiest and the unluckiest. Think of people who are worse off than yourself. Aren't many of them striving bravely to overcome their tremendous difficulties? You can carry a still heavier burden if you try. Since you must be at least partly responsible for your present situation, reflect upon yourself and try to find what is wrong with your way of doing things. The combination also suggests a possibility of a helping hand being extended from above. You should never give up hope.

If you are a woman, you may be troubled by what other people are saying about you. But remember, it all started from a little lie you told before. In a love affair, you may be faced with a difficult situation which is apt to make you desperate, but what you need now is self-criticism. Reflect on your own faults, and don't act desperately and ruin yourself. Avoid solitude, try to smile, and do your best to emerge gradually from your unhappy position. You may count on assistance from your seniors. If you are a man, you are considered a little frivolous and unreliable though agreeable on the surface. Avoid irresponsible talk and try to be sincere. With respect to your health, you tend to drink too much and commit excesses. You need rest rather than medicine.

Although all doors are closed at present, you may be able to improve the situation soon with enough effort, and with assistance from other people. Refer to your index variation to see what is in store for you in a more distant future.

GENERAL: Your efforts are not producing much effect, and you are not trusted by others. Ask a reliable senior or superior for proper advice.

WISHES: It will not be realized immediately. You need the help of a high personage.

TAKU-ZAN-KAN

MARRIAGE: After a temporary break, you will marry him (her) through the medium of a superior. It will be a good match.

BIRTH: Safe. But imprudence might result in a premature rupture of the fetal membrane.

HEALTH: Be temperate in drinking and eating. You might have a fish bone stuck in your throat, or a toothache.

NEGOTIATIONS, DISPUTES: You will be annoyed by prolonged negotiations.

TRAVELING: Wherever you go, you will be in trouble. Cancel the trip.

MISSING PROPERTY: It will be hard to find.

AWAITED PERSONS, MESSAGES: Your interest is not shared by the other party.

MONEY: You will be disappointed. Any speculation will bring you disaster. Don't gamble. You will never win.

MARKET: After staying at a low level for some time, it will fall further.

INDEX VARIATIONS:

1st place:	Da-I-Taku	●○○●○○
2nd place:	Taku-Chi-Sui	●○○●●●
3rd place:	San-Rai-I	○●●●●○
4th place:	Kan-I-Sui	●○●●○●
5th place:	Rai-Sui-Kai	●●○●○●
6th place:	Ten-Sui-Sho	○○○●○●

15. Taku-Zan-Kan ●○○ ○●● A Loving Heart.

BOOK OF CHANGES: *Kan* means sensitivity or flair. Your sixth sense is active, and you are in the right frame of mind for whatever you intend to do. Your luck is capital.

COMMENTS: Whatever you wish will come true. An unexpected happy development is forthcoming. You will be successful in business, in conducting negotiations, in making sales, in everything, especially with the help of superiors.

If you are a man, approach the woman of your heart with sincerity, and she will respond gladly. You may look forward to a happy marriage, and your new home will be warm and constructive. You will be successful in getting a job or entering a school. With a good flair, you will do well in games as well as in business regardless of your normal limitations. But don't wish for things disproportionate with your standing.

If you are a woman, you may be a sensitive dreamer, a buxom, fair-skinned, sweet girl—the type that arouses mens' protective instinct. If you are expecting to marry, don't waste time. If you hesitate, inconveniences may occur.

GENERAL: You will fare well with assistance and protection from others but may be faced with some malice from envious people. Be careful in dealing with the opposite sex.

WISHES: You will get far better results than you expected.

MARRIAGE: It will be an ideal match. Ask a superior for assistance if you want to facilitate the wedding.

BIRTH: Safe.

HEALTH: You have a little mental strain and are overworked.

NEGOTIATIONS, DISPUTES: A settlement will be made easily. As the other party is rather compromising, a little leadership on your part will help.

TAKU-CHI-SUI

TRAVELING: You will have a wonderful companion. You may be on your honeymoon.

MISSING PROPERTY: Ask a child or a woman.

AWAITED PERSONS, MESSAGES: Coming if you send word or make a call.

MONEY: You will make much and spend much. Your earnings will be greater if you follow a superior's advice. You will be able to borrow money with a superior's guarantee.

MARKET: A little bearish but with promise of an upswing. Start your market operations.

INDEX VARIATIONS:

1st place:	Taku-Ka-Kaku	...... ●○○○●○
2nd place:	Taku-Fu-Tai-Ka	.... ●○○○○●
3rd place:	Taku-Chi-Sui	...... ●○○●●●
4th place:	Sui-Zan-Ken	...... ●○●○●●
5th place:	Rai-San-Sho-Ka	.... ●●○○●●
6th place:	Ten-Zan-Ton	...... ○○○○●●

16. Taku-Chi-Sui ●○○ ●●●

Success in Business.

BOOK OF CHANGES: Symbolizing an energetic carp rising to the Dragon Gate, this combination promises promotion, a pay raise, successful admission to a school, etc.

COMMENTS: You have the strong luck of a carp swimming energetically up stream. The combination also stands for convergence, spelling success in business or successful audience mobilization for radio or television programs or other shows.

Before approaching the Dragon Gate, the carp has traveled through numerous hardships including rapids and cascades. The good luck you have now is no accident but the fruit of your past efforts, for which you are beginning to be rewarded. If you are a company employee, you may expect promotion or a pay raise. Pay more attention to your family and home, and be pious. If you are single, you may look forward to a happy marriage. You may have so many offers that you find it hard to make up your mind, but early action will produce better results. In many ways you are active, sociable and attractive, and some people may call you a sweet talker. Keep this criticism in mind.

The combination also stands for reunion, or meeting someone you have not seen for a long time; and you are likely to visit a hot spring, a beach, or other places associated with water.

GENERAL: With the assistance or protection of a superior or a senior, you are likely to achieve unexpected success. Perhaps you are a little bothered by affection from members of the opposite sex.

WISHES: It is likely to be granted, though there may be some interference from a woman.

MARRIAGE: You will be successful in marrying, but there may be interruptions if you take too much time. You will need a mediator. An arrangement made between you and your prospective spouse is apt to fail later.

BIRTH: A girl will be born safe.

HEALTH: You are healthy at present, but beware of food poisoning, stomach troubles and other complaints from eating and drinking.

NEGOTIATIONS, DISPUTES: You are slightly at a disad-

KA-TEN-TAI-YU

vantage. Seek an early settlement. A new trouble seems to be forthcoming.

TRAVELING: You are likely to go off the beaten track away from home.

MISSING PROPERTY: It may have fallen into someone's hands but will be recovered eventually.

AWAITED PERSONS, MESSAGES: Coming, though late.

MONEY: You will make enough money. A little speculation will be safe, bringing you profits by and by. What would you say to a game of bridge tonight?

MARKET: After much trading, there will be a rise.

INDEX VARIATIONS:

1st place:	Taku-Rai-Zui	......●○○●●○
2nd place:	Taku-Sui-Kon	......●○○●○●
3rd place:	Taku-Zan-Kan	......●○○○●●
4th place:	Sui-Chi-Hi	..........●○●●●●
5th place:	Rai-Chi-Yo	........●●○●●●
6th place:	Ten-Chi-Hi	........○○○●●●

"Fire" ○●○ Combinations

17. Ka-Ten-Tai-Yu ○●○ ○○○ The Queen.

BOOK OF CHANGES: You will have the luck of finding a beautiful lily in a deep valley.

COMMENTS: Tai-yu means generosity and fairness, which are among the essential qualities of a wise man respected by the public. The combination stands for freedom, and also symbolizes the sun shining brightly in the firmament. You will be very lucky in spiritual rather than material fields. You will be successful in entering a school, getting a job, or starting a new project. If you have not been doing very well, trust in your ability and brace up. Act aggressively to find your way to success. Leave details to others and put yourself in the position of a commander, who gives orders. But you are likely to lose friends by thinking light of them, and you may have some trouble with close relations, colleagues, or women. If you act too aggressively on the strength of your good luck, you will smart for it later.

If you are a woman, you may have an aptitude for business and be smarter than most men. As an office girl, you may be regarded with some awe by young men working in the same office because you are so smart. Never mind them and relax. Soon a worthy man will ask your hand.

If you are a man, you have caliber, and will be promoted to a responsible position before long.

GENERAL: You will be very successful in spiritual or academic fields. You will be lucky in other fields, too, but you may tend to go too far in seeking an objective.

WISHES: It will not come true if your aim is too high. Wish for things proportionate to your standing.

MARRIAGE: Wedding bells will ring after a little delay. If you are a woman, remember that impatience will undo everything.

BIRTH: See your doctor at an early date.

HEALTH: Beware of fevers, which could be dangerous.

NEGOTIATIONS, DISPUTES: You will succeed if you act aggressively.

KA-TAKU-KEI

TRAVELING: You will have a successful trip if you follow the advice of a senior.

MISSING PROPERTY: It will be found at a high place, or near a shrine or a church.

AWAITED PERSONS, MESSAGES: Coming upon another appeal from you.

MONEY: You will spend a lot. A small sum may be borrowed.

MARKET: A temporary halt will be followed by a rise.

INDEX VARIATIONS:

1st place:	Ka-Fu-Tei	○●○○○●
2nd place:	Ri-I-Ka	○●●○○○
3rd place:	Ka-Taku-Kei	○●○●○○
4th place:	San-Ten-Tai-Chiku	○●●○○○
5th place:	Ken-I-Ten	○○○○○○
6th place:	Rai-Ten-Tai-So	●●○○○○

18. Ka-Taku-Kei

○●○ ●○○ Opposition Without Reason.

BOOK OF CHANGES: You have opposition everywhere. Kei means to rebel or disagree. Be careful of what you say and do if you want to stay out of trouble.

COMMENTS: The combination symbolizes two women glaring at each other with hostility. The situation is fraught with dark passion, as in a triangle. Teamwork is impossible, and an argument develops over the slightest issue. When you say yes, the other party invariably says no, and vice versa. New plans and marriage proposals stand no chance of success. Well-meant advice is regarded with suspicion, and you cannot concentrate on whatever you are doing, vaguely imagining that your superior may have some prejudice against you. You have had many mistakes and troubles, and you have tended to spend carelessly. You are likely to be worked up into an argument and may even hurt someone.

If a man obtains this combination with respect to a woman, his luck cannot be worse. Unless he is extremely careful, he is likely to suffer a great deal on her account, getting something much worse than a mere broken heart.

However, this combination is a lucky one so far as small matters are concerned. Arguments over trivial issues often lead to harmony, as between a man and wife who are always quarreling but actually loving each other.

In any case, try to be modest and listen to your seniors and superiors. There will be a change for the better in three months.

GENERAL: You will suffer much, seeing everything go against your will. Be careful of what you say and do.

WISHES: It is unlikely to come true due to interference.

MARRIAGE: You had better not accept the offer.

BIRTH: Safe, but with disturbing hitches in the schedule.

HEALTH: You had better undergo a close checkup. If you are suffering now, you will do better by changing your doctor. Beware of traffic accidents.

NEGOTIATIONS, DISPUTES: Flexibility will bring you success in making sales or in such other business. If you have a traffic accident with another motorist, talk

RI-I-KA

peacefully. Unnecessary provocation will make the matter worse.

MISSING PROPERTY: It may be found if you look for it in a hurry.

AWAITED PERSONS, MESSAGES: Your suspicion is dampening the enthusiasm of the other party (parties).

MONEY: Save now to provide for the future. You will tend to spend more than you make.

MARKET: There will be an abnormal soar, which will not last.

INDEX VARIATIONS:

1st place:	Ka-Sui-Bi-Sai	......○●○●○●
2nd place:	Ka-Rai-Zei-Go	....○●○●●○
3rd place:	Ka-Ten-Tai-Yu	....○●○○○○
4th place:	San-Taku-Son	......○●●●○○
5th place:	Ten-Taku-Ri	........○○○●○○
6th place:	Rai-Taku-Ki-Mai	....●●○●○○

19. Ri-I-Ka ○●○ ○●○ Overflowing Passion.

BOOK OF CHANGES: The pheasant caught in a net is getting away. Don't rejoice in vain.

COMMENTS: *Ri* means beauty. Your situation is attractive on the surface but poor inside. Happiness seems to be almost here but never comes as troubles occur at the last minute. Also, you might be separated from dear friends or be tricked by others.

In any case, you will see things change frequently and will have to act accordingly, now advancing, now retreating. Conduct yourself with prudence whatever happens. If you receive tempting proposals, regard them with reservations, leaving yourself room for turning back, for you may be disappointed or cheated.

Before accepting a seemingly nice proposition, study the proposal objectively, and ask a third party for advice.

If you are a woman, you may be pretty and tend to seek splendor. You may be a little frivolous and vulnerable to tricks. You need a good advisor. A mistress may have a break with her master.

GENERAL: You will be successful in carrying out things handed over from others. Your luck is strong, but often so strong that you lose prudence, resulting in dangerous turns in your fortune. Over-reliance on your brain may bring you disaster.

WISHES: It will be realized with the help of a senior. You will be successful in anything related to letters, such as literature, academic papers, examinations, printing, and journalism.

MARRIAGE: You had better not marry for the moment. There will be more than one proposal and you will find it hard to make up your mind.

BIRTH: Safe. You might have female twins.

HEALTH: You may have an acute illness, and your condition may deteriorate quickly.

NEGOTIATIONS, DISPUTES: You are likely to end up with no settlement worked out. Ask a friend to mediate.

TRAVELING: Put off the trip if you can.

MISSING PROPERTY: It may be in a beautiful place. Or it may be found unexpectedly if you ask a woman without delay.

AWAITED PERSONS, MESSAGES: Coming.

MONEY: You will lose a little money. If you want to borrow money, ask a friend.

MARKET: There will be a double rise.

KA-RAI-ZEI-GO

20. Ka-Rai-Zei-Go

○●○ ●●○ A Started Engine.

BOOK OF CHANGES: You are bothered by something between your teeth. Crunch it down, and you will feel fine.

COMMENTS: With something weighing on your mind, you feel unhappy day after day. Take resolute action, and you will see things improve gradually. Don't be impatient but proceed with moderation. You will find the bluebird just within your reach.

This combination, like No. 19 (Ri-I-Ka), spells strong luck but without the latter's ominous implications. You will be especially lucky in business. A newly-launched business will go well after some initial difficulties.

If you are a woman, you may be the masculine type and probably tend to talk too much. You may be a group leader who likes to take action. But you may lack tenderness and romantic qualities and may not be liked by men. You are likely to have difficulty in marrying.

GENERAL: You are a little impatient now as things are

not exactly as you wish them to be. But resolute action will remove all obstacles. Whatever happens, proceed bravely.

WISHES: It will not come true immediately due to interference from someone.

MARRIAGE: There will be troubles between you and your prospective spouse, plus unfriendly relatives on the latter's side or hidden enemies, making things generally go wrong.

BIRTH: The child will be born without difficulty, but the mother will suffer from morning sickness. It will be a boy. A balanced diet will be important.

HEALTH: A nervous breakdown or hysteria will linger. You may have a bad tooth. If you have a car of your own, drive carefully. There may be an accident, though it will not be a serious one.

NEGOTIATIONS, DISPUTES: There will be more complication if you have a mediator. Be careful not to be sued.

TRAVELING: You will be safe if you return home quickly, though you may have a minor unpleasantness like an argument.

MISSING PROPERTY: You will find it between or beneath certain things.

AWAITED PERSONS, MESSAGES: Not coming due to difficulties. But you may have some chance if you send word.

MONEY: Money will come and go, never staying in your hands.

MARKET: Some amount of selling will keep the prices down for the moment, but they will gradually go up despite, or just because of, the selling.

INDEX VARIATIONS:

    1st place: Ka-Chi-Shin .... ○●○●●●

KA-FU-TEI

2nd place:	Ka-Taku-Kei	...... ○●○●○○
3rd place:	Ri-I-Ka	.... ○●○○●○
4th place:	San-Rai-I	.... ○●●●●○
5th place:	Ten-Rai-Bu-Mo	.... ○○○●●○
6th place:	Shin-I-Rai	.... ●●○●●○

21. Ka-Fu-Tei

○●○ ○○● Three Arrows.

BOOK OF CHANGES: The tripod (*tei*) is a noble object in China, symbolizing the Imperial Throne. You will be lucky as a leader.

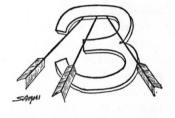

COMMENTS: To maximize your luck, you should abandon the old and adopt the new. With prudence, you will see all your efforts bringing you proper rewards. You will find new friends, and you will succeed if you start anew with new plans. You will be favored by your superiors and achieve prominence. Form a trio with others, for things you cannot do single-handed may be done by the combined effort of three. You have affinity to the number "3." If you are expecting to marry, a step-mother will help. If you insist on living alone with your spouse, a third person may appear to form a triangle with you two, unless you have a baby pretty soon.

Since the combination promises you leadership, you should take the lead in anything. If you are a company employee, you will soon be promoted to a responsible position. If you are a businessman, you may achieve unexpected success on something new. Your residence may be changed.

KA-SUI-BI-SAI

GENERAL: Wait a little while until the time comes. Soon you will be prosperous on a steady basis.

WISHES: It will come true—but possibly with a result somewhat different from what you wanted at first. Cooperation from others will be essential for your success.

MARRIAGE: He (she) is eager, and waiting for your answer. You will marry successfully.

BIRTH: Be careful after the confinement. If the child is your first, it will be a boy; if second, a girl.

HEALTH: You will be in an unsteady state. Beware of fevers and brain diseases.

NEGOTIATIONS, DISPUTES: Use an intermediary for an amicable settlement.

TRAVELING: Don't go on a showy trip. Something unfortunate may happen back home.

MISSING PROPERTY: It is somewhere high and hard to find.

AWAITED PERSONS, MESSAGES: Coming.

MONEY: You will spend a lot of money on a hobby or a pleasure. You will be able to borrow money, but not as much as you want.

MARKET: Balanced.

INDEX VARIATIONS:

1st place:	Ka-Ten-Tai-Yu	....○●○○○○
2nd place:	Ka-Zan-Ryo	........○●●○○●●
3rd place:	Ka-Sui-Bi-Sai	......○●○●○●
4th place:	San-Pu-Ko	........○●●○○●
5th place:	Ten-Pu-Ko	........○○○○○●
6th place:	Rai-Fu-Ko	..........●●○○○●

22. Ka-Sui-Bi-Sai ○●○ ●○● The Wife is an Heiress.

BOOK OF CHANGES: *Bi-Sai* means "not yet accomplished," which is another way of saying your wish will be fulfilled when the time comes. Whereas *Sui-Ka-Ki-Sai* (No. 43) augurs an end, the present combination promises a beginning.

COMMENTS: Your future is full of promise, and you are heading for success. But you are just starting on your way to happiness. Since it is still premature to take aggressive action, proceed slowly and carefully without losing patience. Things will turn increasingly favorable for you.

Perhaps you wish to say something but are not sure whether you should or not.

If you are a woman, you may look forward to a happy event. Youth is the keynote of this combination. An aging man may be attracted to a young woman, a Lolita, a green fruit. But aren't you too old for her? And she isn't a nice girl at that.

GENERAL: Your luck will snowball in time, getting increasingly better as you go on.

WISHES: It will come true, but not immediately.

MARRIAGE: It is a good match. Get married without delay.

BIRTH: A girl will be born safe.

HEALTH: The patient will get better day by day.

NEGOTIATIONS, DISPUTES: You will be at a disadvantage. If you are involved in a dispute, you had better give in.

TRAVELING: A long trip had better be canceled.

MISSING PROPERTY: You left it somewhere. It will not be recovered.

AWAITED PERSONS, MESSAGES: Not coming due to a difficulty.

MONEY: With a lot of spending, your position will be insecure.

MARKET: An upturn will follow minor fluctuations.

KA-ZAN-RYO

INDEX VARIATIONS:

1st place:	Ka-Taku-Kei	......○●●○○○
2nd place:	Ka-Chi-Shin	........○●●●●●
3rd place:	Ka-Fu-Tei	........○●○○○●
4th place:	San-Sui-Mo	........○●●●○●
5th place:	Ten-Sui-Sho	........○○○●○●
6th place:	Rai-Sui-Kai	........●●○●○●

23. Ka-Zan-Ryo ○●○ ○●● A Lone Traveler.

BOOK OF CHANGES: A traveler on a long journey is unsettled, weary, and lonely.

COMMENTS: *Ryo* means traveling. You are a belated traveler, weary both physically and mentally after a long day's journey, looking for a place to lodge for the night. The lucky spell you have had is coming to an end, leaving you in a somewhat insecure state. Perhaps you are sullen, unsociable, and solitary—a disposition suited for academic or literary pursuits. You will have trouble with your residence (beware of fire), and tend to be out of home.

The combination spells good luck for businessmen and students going abroad. In any case, it is important for you to be passive at all times. Aggressive action will bring you misfortune. A seemingly attractive proposition will turn out to be disappointing, much to your frustration. You will be lonely, proceeding alone, and you may be separated from your spouse against your will. Marriage will be difficult for you as you frequently move from one residence to another and switch from one job to another. Refer to your index variation to see what will happen in the more distant future.

Incidentally, the author got this combination with

respect to Mrs. Jacqueline Kennedy. She is likely to take a job outside the U.S.

GENERAL: You are haunted by an irritating sensation that something unfortunate is following you, threatening to catch up, as you continue to trudge along. Stop worrying. What will happen will happen. But remember to be passive at all times.

You will be successful in academic pursuits or in seeking admission to a school.

WISHES: It will be partly fulfilled. But don't ask too much, or you will lose all.

MARRIAGE: You will marry, but the marriage will not last long.

BIRTH: There will be troubles.

HEALTH: There will be a lull, but the condition is serious.

NEGOTIATIONS, DISPUTES: You will get a better settlement by putting it off.

TRAVELING: You will be lucky on an overseas trip. Other trips had better be canceled.

MISSING PROPERTY: It will be found if you look for it at once. It is in a high place, or in the South.

AWAITED PERSONS, MESSAGES: Coming late.

MONEY: You will spend much on a hobby or in relations with the opposite sex. A little money may be made.

MARKET: The trend is upward, but there will be a fall at a later time.

INDEX VARIATIONS:

1st place:	Ri-I-Ka	○●○○○●
2nd place:	Ka-Fu-Tei	○●○○○●
3rd place:	Ka-Chi-Shin	○●○●●●
4th place:	Gon-I-Zan	○●●○●●
5th place:	Ten-Zan-Ton	○○○○●●

KA-CHI-SHIN

6th place: Rai-San-Sho-Ka ....●●○○●●
24. Ka-Chi-Shin ○●○ ●●● Fight for Success.

BOOK OF CHANGES: The sun is up above the horizon. With the patronage of a senior or a superior, you will grab a chance for success. Your luck is rising.

COMMENTS: The combination symbolizes the rising sun above the horizon, casting more and more light on everything around you. You will be increasingly lucky and enjoy general prosperity. You will be favored by your superior and stand a good chance of promotion. You will meet with an old friend, old lover, or make up with an old enemy.

Since *Shin* means advance, you should go ahead counting on your luck. The signal has turned green. But don't be conceited or idle, or Fortune will turn away from you. As the combination may also be interpreted to indicate a state magnificent outside and empty inside, try to be moderate and industrious. That is how you can make capital of your luck. Also, you should be prepared for considerable jealousy and obstruction from others.

GENERAL: Proceed with confidence to achieve your objectives. Your luck is on the rise.

WISHES: With a little delay, it will come true to your satisfaction.

MARRIAGE: The proposition is sound. About your new home and wedding, consult your mother or aunt.

BIRTH: Safe.

HEALTH: You will have a slight ailment, which might be dangerous if you are old.

NEGOTIATIONS, DISPUTES: Positive action on your part will facilitate a settlement.

RAI-TEN-TAI-SO

TRAVELING: You will have no trouble.

MISSING PROPERTY: It has been carried far away.

AWAITED PERSONS, MESSAGES: Good news will be brought to you.

MONEY: You will spend much, but it will pay off handsomely.

MARKET: There will be a rise. As the market is at a turning point, consider all factors carefully and act accordingly. You will earn a lot.

INDEX VARIATIONS:

1st place:	Ka-Rai-Zei-Go	....○●○●●○
2nd place:	Ka-Sui-Bi-Sai	......○●○●○●
3rd place:	Ka-Zan-Ryo	........○●○○●●
4th place:	San-Chi-Haku	......○●●●●○
5th place:	Ten-Chi-Hi	........○○○●●●
6th place:	Rai-Chi-Yo	........●●○○●●

"Thunder" ●●○ Combinations

25. Rai-Ten-Tai-So

●●○ ○○○ Use the Brakes Too.

BOOK OF CHANGES: The thunder rumbles loudly across the sky. It sounds grand, but does not always bring rain.

COMMENTS: The mid-summer sun beats fiercely on the ground and everything seems heaving heavily, when suddenly you hear a clap of thunder promising long-awaited rain. But rain never comes.

In a way the thunder symbolizes you, loud, over-powering, virile—Indeed so powerful that you are oppressing everyone around you. Don't be too wilful if you want to stay lucky. Don't venture forward reck-lessly. To be sure, your luck is on the rise. Fortune will smile on you if you behave properly. But if you rely too much on your smartness or money and make light of others, you may draw the wrath of a superior or otherwise bring misfortune on yourself. Be ambitious, but proceed with modesty. If you do, you will be suc-cessful in business.

If you are a woman, you may hold a good position in business. You are rather masculine, open-minded and cheerful, calculative and sharp, but unfortunately, a little stubborn and coarse, which is why you have not been very lucky in finding a good husband. Within six months, however, you will receive an acceptable proposal. In seasonal terms, this combination re-presents February.

GENERAL: Don't go too far if you want to avoid misfor-tune. Use the brakes properly. You will be lucky in gambling. You are likely to have a traffic accident. You will not be hurt much, but your car will be heavily damaged.

WISHES: It will be granted if you are modest.

MARRIAGE: The match-maker's information may be unreliable. There is some possibility of an unfavorable extramarital relationship.

BIRTH: Stay on guard, or you will have a surprise. More likely than not, it will be safe.

RAI-TAKU-KI-MAI

HEALTH: You may have a sudden attack of illness. If your blood pressure is high, avoid sleeplessness, heavy drinking, and constipation.

NEGOTIATIONS, DISPUTES: The other party is likely to get away unhurt. Try not to be stubborn.

TRAVELING: Misfortune may await you where you are going. It would be wise to cancel the trip.

MISSING PROPERTY: It has been carried far away. It will not be recovered.

AWAITED PERSONS, MESSAGES: Coming, possibly with a companion.

MONEY: You will spend much outside. You will hear of possible loans, but you will not be able to borrow any money.

MARKET: Bullish.

INDEX VARIATIONS:

1st place:	Rai-Fu-Ko	●●○○○●
2nd place:	Rai-Ka-Ho	●●○○●○
3rd place:	Rai-Taku-Ki-Mai	●●○●○○
4th place:	Chi-Ten-Tai	●●●○○○
5th place:	Taku-Ten-Kai	●○○○○○
6th place:	Ka-Ten-Tai-Yu	○●○○○○

26. Rai-Taku-Ki-Mai ●●○ ●○○ The Forbidden Fruit.

BOOK OF CHANGES: Heaven and Earth, positive and negative, man and woman, are locked in an esctatic embrace. Your love will be consummated. But remember, you have to begin well.

COMMENTS: This combination symbolizes a girl chasing a man. The picture looks happy, but having made the wrong start, you are likely to be disappointed in your expectations and suffer. You will be irritated and frustrated on many occasions. Whatever you do, proceed with care.

If you are a man, you are liable to fall in trouble with a woman. Keep away from women for the moment. Nothing in the world are more dangerous than women. You may also have trouble with your wife.

The situation is not so unfavorable if you are a woman, although you have to remember that the relationship you may have with a man is likely to be carnal rather than legal—you may not be marrying formally. If you want marriage, you should go right ahead if you are marrying for the second time, but had better wait a little more if it is going to be your first marriage. There is a high possibility of your becoming a sort of mistress. Unless you are prepared to accept such status, don't plunge into anything emotionally. It is most important for you to start well. The signal is not red but amber. Proceed with caution, whether in business or in dealing with a person. You should be passive rather than active, and always act carefully.

GENERAL: Things look favorable at first but may become less so as you go on. Be passive. You may suffer injustice, be frustrated, or have an unpleasant surprise.

WISHES: It will take time, due to some hindrance.

MARRIAGE: Be careful in dealing with the opposite sex. You may be in a triangle. Perhaps you may have already stepped across the last line. The prospect is unfavorable if you are marrying for the first time, but favorable if it is going to be your second marriage.

BIRTH: A boy will be born safe.

HEALTH: An old illness may return.

RAI-KA-HO

NEGOTIATIONS, DISPUTES: There may be a breach of promise or an unfortunate development.

TRAVELING: Cancel the trip unless you are going on business. A trip with your lover is likely to bring about unhappy consequences.

MISSING PROPERTY: A woman is involved.

AWAITED PERSONS, MESSAGES: Not coming soon. But you will get response if you send word.

MONEY: You will earn much less than you spend. You may be able to borrow money from a woman, but there will be trouble later on.

MARKET: The rise will be checked by new unfavorable factors, and the market will turn somewhat bearish.

INDEX VARIATIONS:

1st place:	Rai-Sui-Kai	........●●○○●●
2nd place:	Shin-I-Rai	........●●○●●○
3rd place:	Rai-Ten-Tai-So	....●●○○○○
4th place:	Chi-Taku-Rin	......●●●●○○
5th place:	Dai-I-Taku	........●○○●○○
6th place:	Ka-Taku-Kei	......○●○●○○

27. Rai-Ka-Ho

●●○ ○●○ Harvest Time.

BOOK OF CHANGES: Opulence is the keynote of your strongly lucky state.

COMMENTS: Your luck is as strong as a bolt cracking across the sky, although behind the prosperous appearance there may be hidden troubles. In Yi augury, strength is not all that you require for success. Despite your

strong luck, carelessness or imprudence may bring you into trouble with other people, possibly resulting in unhappy situations.

You may look forward to succeed in the electrical business. If you are a farmer, you will have a bumper crop.

If you are doing well right now, you will go a long way further. But remember, a full moon is bound to wane. Don't expand too much, but try to save and seek internal improvement.

If you are in the entertainment or cultural field, you will get along very well. Proceed without hesitation. Perhaps you will have additional success in some side-line.

If you are a woman, you may be a voluptuous beauty, but you may also be prolific.

GENERAL: You appear to be in a grand state but seem to be a little impatient. There may be troubles in store for you.

WISHES: It looks promising but may not be very fruitful.

MARRIAGE: The proposal is attractive on the surface but may not bring you much in practice. Make thorough investigations lest you should be sorry later.

BIRTH: Best care is required after the confinement. The baby will be born without trouble.

HEALTH: A slight ailment, without proper care, may develop into a chronic disease.

NEGOTIATIONS, DISPUTES: You will win if you think quick and decide quick. Don't ask too much. If you are a salesman in an electrical business, you may land a big order.

TRAVELING: You may go if you expect to return soon. But the best thing to do is not to go.

SHIN-I-RAI

MISSING PROPERTY: It will not be recovered.

AWAITED PERSONS, MESSAGES: Not coming immediately. There will be a delay.

MONEY: You will do well.

MARKET: It will hit the peak pretty soon, and a decline will follow.

INDEX VARIATIONS:

1st place:	Rai-San-Sho-Ka	●●○○●●
2nd place:	Rai-Ten-Tai-So	●●○○○○
3rd place:	Shin-I-Rai	●●○●●○
4th place:	Chi-Ka-Mei-I	●●●○●○
5th place:	Taku-Ka-Kaku	●○○○●○
6th place:	Ri-I-Ka	○●○○●○

28. Shin-I-Rai ●●○ ●●○ Promise Without Substance.

BOOK OF CHANGES: Two mighty dragons are contending for a single jewel. You see it almost within your reach, but never get it.

COMMENTS: The situation looks most favorable, promising you success. But you have a competitor, and the competition keeps you from getting hold of what you are after. Moreover, it may turn out to be insubstantial when you finally get it.

Your plans and ambitions will bring you nothing unless you follow the advice of your seniors and superiors.

But proper judgement, decision, and effort, coupled with assistance from superiors, will enable you to achieve prominence. Perhaps you may succeed to the headship of a prestigious group. Anger may cause you to lose something.

There will be a surprising development around you

shortly, but it will not harm you much. Remember that good advice is often unpalatable.

If you are expecting to marry, you are likely to have a rival, another dragon trying to grab the same jewel. If it is going to be your first marriage, don't count too much on it.

GENERAL: With a good cooperator, you will go a very long way.

WISHES: It looks almost coming true but never does.

MARRIAGE: It will not be a very good match if you are marrying for the first time. Otherwise, you can expect to be happily married.

BIRTH: There will be a little trouble.

HEALTH: An old illness is likely to recur. Beware of hypertension.

NEGOTIATIONS, DISPUTES: You are at an advantage. Be patient.

TRAVELING: There will be a surprise away from home.

MISSING PROPERTY: It will not be recovered for the time being.

AWAITED PERSONS, MESSAGES: The one closer to you will come later than the more distant one.

MONEY: You will lose more than you make. You will be luckier later.

MARKET: A double rise will be followed by a sharp decline. You will lose heavily if you go too far.

INDEX VARIATIONS:

1st place:	Rai-Chi-Yo	●●○●●●
2nd place:	Rai-Taku-Ki-Mai	●●○●○○
3rd place:	Rai-Ka-Ho	●●○○●○
4th place:	Chi-Rai-Fuku	●●●●●○
5th place:	Taku-Rai-Zui	●○○●●○

RAI-FU-KO

6th place: Ka-Rai-Zei-Go ....○●○●●○
29. Rai-Fu-Ko

●●○ ○○● Suppressed
Desires.

BOOK OF CHANGES: Two forces are in line but working in opposite directions. There will be opposition to anything new.

COMMENTS: Everything will go well so long as you live as you have always been. To escape boredom, however, you are tempted to seek something new or exciting.

But don't venture on anything new at this moment, whether it is a new project, a new business operation, or new negotiations; and don't try to hurry with whatever you are doing right now, for you will soon be out of breath and compelled to give it up. Wait until the signal turns green. Stay where you are.

In matrimonial relations, your spouse may be irritable with suppressed desires. Don't think you don't have to feed the fish you have already hooked. A storm will be forthcoming unless you are nice to your spouse as well as to every one else. A common-law marriage may fail.

Whether you are lucky or unlucky at this moment, the trend is likely to be reversed after a while. By seeking a change, you will be asking for trouble.

GENERAL: You will get along if you stay passive, refraining from acting on your own initiative. Be imaginative and ingenious in dealing with others.

WISHES: It will be granted if you don't hurry.

RAI-SUI-KAI

MARRIAGE: Neither you nor the other party is very enthusiastic, but it would not be a bad match. But a common-law marriage may fail.

BIRTH: A girl will be born safe.

HEALTH: Beware of chronic ailments, such as gout, neuralgia, and indigestion.

NEGOTIATIONS, DISPUTES: It will take time to achieve a settlement. You would be better off if you gave it up for the moment.

TRAVELING: You had better not go on a long trip.

MISSING PROPERTY: It will be found very close to you.

AWAITED PERSONS, MESSAGES: Coming late due to an interruption on the way.

MONEY: You will be rather lucky in making money.

MARKET: There will be a departure from the balanced state. Get ready now.

INDEX VARIATIONS:

1st place:	Rai-Ten-Tai-So	....	●●○○○○
2nd place:	Rai-San-Sho-Ka	....	●●○○●●
3rd place:	Rai-Sui-Kai	....	●●○●○●
4th place:	Chi-Fu-Sho	....	●●●○○●
5th place:	Taku-Fu-Tai-Ka	....	●○○○○●
6th place:	Ka-Fu-Tei	....	○●○○○●

30. Rai-Sui-Kai ●●○ ●○● A Thaw.

BOOK OF CHANGES: With the cold ice melting, everything is coming to life again. Old problems and worries will be solved.

COMMENTS: After a long period of hardship, you are now heading for success. Your problems will be solved, and happiness will be yours if you grab this chance and venture forward. But you need quick decision and action. You will miss the chance if you are slow as you have often been in the past. Though things are generally in your favor, don't squander money or spare effort. If you are indulgent, the tables may be turned on you once again.

This combination foretells separation as well as solution and liberation. Try to be cooperative. If you are engaged, you had better marry without delay.

It also symbolizes "sailing far," or a couple of followers cooperating to help their master out of a mess. You will be successful in trade business, and you will benefit from encouragement or good ideas from your subordinates or colleagues.

GENERAL: Grabbing a chance, you will make a great advance. You may look forward to going abroad.

WISHES: Old wishes will come true. New wishes will take time.

MARRIAGE: With more time lost, the proposal will be dropped.

BIRTH: A boy will be born safe.

HEALTH: The patient will be safe. If you are a woman, you may have skin eruptions.

NEGOTIATIONS, DISPUTES: Be honest, and hurry. Bargaining will do you more harm than good.

TRAVELING: You will have some happy development on the trip, such as meeting an old friend who will help you expand your business.

MISSING PROPERTY: It will be found at a high place unless it was stolen.

AWAITED PERSONS, MESSAGES: Coming if you call.

MONEY: You will have a chance to make a fortune.

MARKET: After staying low, the market is looking up again.

RAI-SAN-SHO-KA

INDEX VARIATIONS:

1st place: Rai-Taku-Ki-Mai .... ●●○●○○
2nd place: Rai-Chi-Yo ....●●○●●●
3rd place: Rai-Fu-Ko ....●●○○○●
4th place: Chi-Sui-Shi ....●●●●○●
5th place: Taku-Sui-Kon ......●○○●○●
6th place: Ka-Sui-Bi-Sai ......○●○●○●

31. Rai-San-Sho-Ka ●●○ ○●● The Chance is Gone.

BOOK OF CHANGES: There will be a little excess, a minor error.

COMMENTS: You are like the hunter chasing a flying bird, eyes skyward, eager, impatient, unaware of the bog at your feet. Hot after the game, you will soon be lost in the woods. Careful preparations and discreet action are essential for success. If someone asks a favor of you, don't say "yes" carelessly, or you will be in trouble later. Some people will turn against you, and you will have a lot of things to worry about.

This combination also foretells "departure from home."

A small man will have a temptation to do something wrong. Heedless of the dangers involved, he may be blinded by the prospect of fabulous gains and ruin himself.

Even you will do well if you try to be conservative, modest, and conciliatory with others.

On a date, don't be impatient if she (he) does not share what you feel. She (he) is not thinking of you right now. Perhaps both of you have been a little too self-assertive. A cooling off period will do much good. If you hurry to win her (his) heart back, you will end up losing it.

You will have some marriage proposals, but they will amount to little.

GENERAL: You may be doing badly now, but a chance is forthcoming. Grab it with a cool head.

WISHES: It seems almost coming true but will not be realized easily. You have lost the best chance for it.

MARRIAGE: You will have no luck, with problems cropping up over trivial matters. After a lot of talk, you will be no closer to the goal.

BIRTH: There will be a little delay, and the baby may be sickly.

HEALTH: The ailment will not be dangerous but may linger without proper care. There may be some tendency to impotence, due to excesses.

NEGOTIATIONS, DISPUTES: With both parties staying adamant, settlement seems far off. Perhaps you should make some concessions.

TRAVELING: You may fall a victim to illness or robbery on the trip. You had better not go. Also, there may be loss of virginity.

MISSING PROPERTY: It will be found near water, or somewhere north in the house, though your chance of finding it is not very high.

AWAITED PERSONS, MESSAGES: You will hear from him (her), but he (she) is not ready to come.

MONEY: Perhaps you should economize a little at home. There is a glowing prospect of making money, but you are likely to end up losing some. Beware of seemingly attractive propositions.

MARKET: Generally there will be little change, but you will make some immediate gains by clever buying or selling. Don't stay long in the game.

RAI-CHI-YO

INDEX VARIATIONS:

32. Rai-Chi-Yo ●●○ ●●● Ready to Start.

BOOK OF CHANGES: The Thunder Deity now ascends to Heaven. Spring is coming to bring everything back to life.

COMMENTS: Happiness and joy will be yours if you seek success with adequate preparations. Your luck is vigorously on the rise. After staying low for a long time, you are going to fare well. But don't go too far, counting too much on your luck, or misfortune may take you by surprise. Watch your step lest you stumble. Be careful of what you say.

Now you have a keen sense of what is forthcoming. Perhaps you will be able to work out successful business plans. You are sure to win in poker and other games. You will be successful in a new business venture, provided you make sufficient preliminary research and preparations. Once on your way to success, straighten out your agreements, contracts, and other arrangements to avoid future trouble.

Marriage will make you happy. The family you are marrying into is a little untidy, but you will set things right. If you are a woman, probably you are sweet and bright.

GENERAL: Following your objectives in good order, you

will be very successful. Indulgence in leisure pursuits will not do you good. Even with best luck, you will eventually lose if you stay too long in the game. Beware of temptations to spend too much time on something besides your main business.

WISHES: It will come true with some delay. It may seem almost lost at times, but will be realized eventually. Be persistent.

MARRIAGE: Positive action will bring you luck. There may be a little complication in the family of your prospective spouse, but it will be nothing serious.

BIRTH: Safe.

HEALTH: A long illness will be cured gradually, but a sudden illness may be dangerous. Consult the doctor at once.

NEGOTIATIONS, DISPUTES: Stay cool if you want to avoid failure.

TRAVELING: You will have a little difficulty in climbing a mountain. You had better go with an older companion or follow a good leader.

MISSING PROPERTY: Give it up. It will not be recovered.

AWAITED PERSONS, MESSAGES: You have to wait awhile. There has been an interruption on the way.

MONEY: You tend to spend more than you make.

MARKET: A rise carried too far will be followed by a fall.

INDEX VARIATIONS:

1st place:	Shin-I-Rai	●●○●●○
2nd place:	Rai-Sui-Kai	●●○●○●
3rd place:	Rai-San-Sho-Ka	●●○○●●
4th place:	Kon-I-Chi	●●●●●●
5th place:	Taku-Chi-Sui	●○○●●●
6th place:	Ka-Chi-Shin	○●○●●●

FU-TEN-SHO-CHIKU

"Wind" OO● Combinations

33. Fu-Ten-Sho-Chiku

OO● OOO Just Drift.

BOOK OF CHANGES: The moon is pale before dawn. Your luck is still low.

COMMENTS: Frailty and instability, symbolized by the pale moon before dawn, characterize the state you are in. When things appear to be going well, a sudden interruption will hinder your progress. The way is not quite clear for you as yet. Whatever you want to do, the time is not mature.

With everything in suspension, you may not be in a happy state of mind. But the impasse is only temporary, and luck will soon return. Be patient.

If you are a woman, you may have saved a little money, perhaps by clever stock market operations. But recently you may be losing a little, having little success in whatever you do. Patience is what you need most at this moment. Wait three months, and you will again be making money, though not much. Besides, some happy developments seem to be forthcoming. With your eagerness for business, you will make a good wife for a store proprietor, for you are a born money-maker.

But too much eagerness for money may give you an unfavorable reputation as a "tightwad."

This combination also suggests female predomin-

FU-TAKU-CHU-BU

ance. A man may be overwhelmed by his wife. But if you are a woman, you can hope to keep your husband well under control.

GENERAL: Your fortunes are being affected by lack of harmony with your spouse. If you are unmarried, you are likely to have trouble with your colleagues or friends.

WISHES: Hindrances tend to occur.

MARRIAGE: After a few unsuccessful attempts, you will hear wedding bells.

BIRTH: There is a possibility of a miscarriage.

HEALTH: The illness is likely to linger with repeated relapses. Beware of nettle rash and neuralgia due to overwork.

NEGOTIATIONS, DISPUTES: Your progress will be hindered temporarily, but impatience will make a mess of everything.

TRAVELING: You had better give up the trip.

MISSING PROPERTY: Will not be recovered.

AWAITED PERSONS, MESSAGES: Not coming in time due to frequent changes in your whereabouts.

MONEY: You will make a little money.

MARKET: Unchanged.

INDEX VARIATIONS:

1st place:	Son-I-Fu	○○●○○●
2nd place:	Fu-Ka-Ka-Jin	○○●○●○
3rd place:	Fu-Taku-Chu-Bu	○○●●○○
4th place:	Ken-I-Ten	○○○○○○
5th place:	San-Ten-Tai-Chiku	○●●○○○
6th place:	Sui-Ten-Ju	●○●○○○

34. Fu-Taku-Chu-Bu ○○● ●○○ In Love.

BOOK OF CHANGES: The hen is nesting, and the eggs will hatch. Cooperation will bear fruit.

COMMENTS: Sincerity and faith will bring great success to an honest, hard-working person. With genuine effort and enthusiasm, anything can be done. Your approaches will be met with favorable response. You will have good luck as a salesman or a negotiator, and very good luck in cooperative undertakings. But the hen is still sitting on the eggs and  should not be disturbed at the present moment if you want them to hatch. So, proceed prudently. With proper care, your business plans or ideas will soon see the light of day.

But just because you are faring well, you will have a lot of temptations. Smooth-tongued crooks must be flatly rejected. Counting too much on your smartness and acting against the advice of your seniors and superiors will bring you disaster. The combination also suggests man and woman in love. Talk to your trusted senior or superior at once, and with his (her) advice or help, get married without delay. You will have a nice baby.

If you are married, you are very happy with your spouse, though there are some temptations in the wife's heart.

GENERAL: Your ability, once recognized, will get you very far. But over-reliance on your smartness will bring disaster. Don't act arbitrarily.

WISHES: It will be yours if sought with sincerity and effort.

FU-KA-KA-JIN

MARRIAGE: Give a free hand to a trusted senior or superior, and you will be happily married. (There is a tendency to inconstancy on the woman's side, but it will not amount to much if the man is broad-minded.)

BIRTH: Safe. Care should be taken after the confinement. If the wife has a habit of miscarriage, the husband's cooperation and understanding is important.

HEALTH: A slight illness casually contracted may get serious. Consult the doctor without delay. Beware of hepatic chirrhosis.

NEGOTIATIONS, DISPUTES: A settlement will be made after long effort but will not bring you as much benefit as you expect.

TRAVELING: Travel by ship.

MISSING PROPERTY: It has been lost among other things.

AWAITED PERSONS, MESSAGES: Coming if you call.

MONEY: Despite the high promise, you will make only about a quarter of what you are expecting. Nevertheless, your chances of making money are favorable.

MARKET: Rising slowly.

INDEX VARIATIONS:

1st place:	Fu-Sui-Kan	○○●●○●
2nd place:	Fu-Rai-Eki	○○●●●○
3rd place:	Fu-Ten-Sho-Chika	○○●○○○
4th place:	Ten-Taku-Ri	○○○●○○
5th place:	San-Taku-Son	○●●●○○
6th place:	Sui-Taku-Setsu	●○●●○○

35. Fu-Ka-Ka-Jin ○○● ○●○ Domestic Peace.

BOOK OF CHANGES: Moonlight begins to stream into the room. Hope rises.

COMMENTS: Your home is comfortable, with everyone

helping to make it so. But your environment is a little feminine and conservative.

Accustomed to peace, you tend to want more excitement, seeking adventure on ambitious propositions. But don't over-reach yourself, and don't venture, if you don't want trouble. Holding your own is the best way to ensure happiness. Generally, you will be lucky at home and unlucky away from home. Trusting in or cooperating with others will bring satisfactory results.

If you are a woman, your husband or fiance is likely to be gentle and sweet, but a little feminine. You miss something. But he is, or will make, a good husband. Though a little soft, he has merits of his own. And you will have nice children. The neighbor's flowers always seem prettier than your own.

GENERAL: Starting in a modest way, you will do increasingly better. Your luck is steadily on the rise.

WISHES: It will be realized with others' cooperation.

MARRIAGE: Ask a kindly woman. She will make all necessary investigations, and you will marry happily.

BIRTH: Safe.

HEALTH: Beware of enervation and impotence.

NEGOTIATIONS, DISPUTES: Things will turn in your favor, though with some complications.

TRAVELING: How about a family vacation trip? It will be a great success.

MISSING PROPERTY: It is in the house, but will not be found readily.

AWAITED PERSONS, MESSAGES: You had better call. If you are expecting to borrow money, ask for it through a woman's medium.

FU-RAI-EKI

MONEY: You will waste much money.
MARKET: A brief rise will be followed by a fall.
INDEX VARIATIONS:

1st place:	Fu-Zan-Zen	........○○●○●●
2nd place:	Fu-Ten-Sho-Chiku	..○○●○○○
3rd place:	Fu-Rai-Eki	........○○●●●○
4th place:	Ten-Ka-Do-Jin	....○○○○●○
5th place:	San-Ka-Hi	..........○●●○●○
6th place:	Sui-Ka-Ki-Sai	......●○●○●○

36. Fu-Rai-Eki ○○● ●●○ Public Interest First.

BOOK OF CHANGES: The time has come for fulfilment.
Your luck is on the high tide. The crop will be bumper.

COMMENTS: There will be a flow of benefit from above
to below, as in a public works project subsidized by
the government and undertaken for the good of the
local public. But you cannot expect immediate personal gains. As a leader you will benefit people around
you, and eventually they will bring you a lot in return.
Your luck is the luck of being able to benefit others.
If you do so with eagerness, you will get their cooperation, which will be both beneficial and pleasant. You
will have much success as a salesman.

If you are a salary-earner, this is the time for a pay
raise or promotion. You will help your fellow-workers
and subordinates and be helped by them. Although
unexpected rumors about you, or a necessity to move,
may make you unhappy, try not to be bothered. A
change of residence, especially, is more advisable than
not.

This combination suggests public works, government
agencies, civil engineering, and agriculture. Anything
in these or related fields will bring you much benefit.

SON-I-FU

If you are a woman, you are likely to serve as a go-between for two lovers, and someone may ask your hand all of a sudden. It will be a good match.

GENERAL: Venture forward for more luck.

WISHES: It will be realized with a superior's help.

MARRIAGE: The proposal is rather sudden, but you will marry in due course.

BIRTH: Safe.

HEALTH: You may be heading for a long illness. Beware of traffic accidents.

NEGOTIATIONS, DISPUTES: You are at an advantage, but the tables may be turned upon you if you lose time. Follow your superiors' suggestions.

TRAVELING: You will be lucky on a business trip. It will be a busy one.

MISSING PROPERTY: Ask a woman. It may or may not be found.

AWAITED PERSONS, MESSAGES: There may be a companion.

MONEY: You will have an unexpected income. You are in for more money.

MARKET: Building and construction stocks will go up. Others will fluctuate, with bullish overtones.

INDEX VARIATIONS:

1st place:	Fu-Chi-Kan	........○○●●●●
2nd place:	Fu-Taku-Chu-Bu	....○○●●○○
3rd place:	Fu-Ka-Ka-Jin	......○○●○●○
4th place:	Ten-Rai-Bu-Mo	......○○○●●○
5th place:	San-Rai-I	..........○●●●●○
6th place:	Sui-Rai-Chun	........●○●●●○

37. Son-I-Fu ○○● ○○● A Wandering Heart.

BOOK OF CHANGES: Acquiesce, follow, and bow as the wind does. A golden chance may be grabbed that way.

COMMENTS: Instead of acting on your own initiative, proceed under the lead of a superior and hop on the bandwagon. You will have much luck in business, although as a salesman you will have to talk much before landing an order.

The combination suggests wandering to and fro, right and left. Without a cool head, you will sometimes find it hard to make up your mind. If you are expecting to marry, especially, things are unlikely to go smoothly. There will be a lot of dilly-dallying on both sides, both feeling vaguely that something better may come up. Insincerity underlying sweet talk, suspicion, and misunderstanding may lead to a catastrophe.

Within 5 months, a good fortune will come through such as good job or inheritance. If you are a salaried man, you will be promoted.

GENERAL: You will fail if you insist on going your own way, and succeed if you cooperate with others.

WISHES: There will be some obstruction. A female intermediary will be useful.

MARRIAGE: There will be a lot of complications.

BIRTH: A boy will be born safe.

HEALTH: The illness may be fatal to an old person but will not do much harm if the patient is young. He (she) will recover pretty soon.

NEGOTIATIONS, DISPUTES: You will be in trouble if you are too aggressive.

TRAVELING: You will be on the trip longer than you expect.

MISSING PROPERTY: Ask a woman. If you still cannot find it, give it up.

AWAITED PERSONS, MESSAGES: Coming. But you will not be there.

FU-SUI-KAN

MONEY: You will not be out of money if you refrain from pretenses and tricks.

MARKET: Balanced, though with minor ups and downs.

INDEX VARIATIONS:

1st place:	Fu-Ten-Sho-Chiku	..○○●○○○
2nd place:	Fu-Zan-Zen	........○○●○●●
3rd place:	Fu-Sui-Kan	........○○●●○●
4th place:	Ten-Pu-Ko	........○○○○○●
5th place:	San-Pu-Ko	..........○●●○○●
6th place:	Sui-Fu-Sei	..........●○●○○●

38. Fu-Sui-Kan

○○● ●○● Sailing Out With Hope.

BOOK OF CHANGES: Sailing smoothly with the wind, you are full of hope, and everything will go as you wish.

COMMENTS: With the spring wind carrying away the cold of winter, the old ice of difficulties is beginning to melt, and hope is rising high. You are getting out of your long unlucky state.

This combination also suggests shipping, and going overseas. You will hear a lot about foreign trade or going abroad to study, giving you a rare opportunity to start anew with high hopes.

Though your future is now bright, don't act recklessly. Reflect on your past and proceed prudently. As another implication of this combination is "scattering," whatever you earn may easily scatter if you don't watch out. Money will come and go, and you will be busy day after day. Eventually you may have a sort of nervous breakdown, forgetting things and neglecting appointments, which will be detrimental to your reputation as a reliable person.

Whether in business or in love, you will fare extremely well, but unexpected troubles may occur if you hurry too much. If you have been a little touchy lately, try to be softer and warmer, like the spring wind. You will find a good adviser. If you are a woman, a secretarial job will be good for you. If you are a man, you will make a successful businessman or politician. Departing from your relatively minor career in the past, you are going to be a big leader.

GENERAL: With your old problems solved, you are starting on a new, hopeful voyage. You will be busy, but will be rewarded handsomely. You are in a position to fully exercise your ability. But don't overdo it, or you will end up losing much money.

WISHES: It will take time, but will be realized eventually if you proceed in good order.

MARRIAGE: You will be able to marry, but watch out for interruptions.

BIRTH: Beware of a miscarriage.

HEALTH: Stay on guard.

NEGOTIATIONS, DISPUTES: Give a free hand to a trusted senior or superior.

TRAVELING: You will be on the trip longer than you expect.

MISSING PROPERTY: Will not be recovered.

AWAITED PERSONS, MESSAGES: Not coming immediately. But good news is forthcoming.

MONEY: You will spend much.

MARKET: After hitting a new high, it will be down again.

FU-ZAN-ZEN

INDEX VARIATIONS:

1st place:	Fu-Taku-Chu-Bu	....○○●●○○
2nd place:	Fu-Chi-Kan	........○○●●●●
3rd place:	Son-I-Fu	.........○○●○○●
4th place:	Ten-Sui-Sho	........○○○●○●
5th place:	San-Sui-Mo	........○●●●○○
6th place:	Kan-I-Sui	.........●○●●○●

39. Fu-Zan-Zen ○○● ○●● Step by Step.

BOOK OF CHANGES: Afforestation promises growth and prosperity.

COMMENTS: You will be increasingly lucky if you proceed step by step in good order. You are very close to promotion or success. Whatever you win next, set your feet firmly on it before climbing higher. Being better off, you will pay more attention to the opposite sex. You are likely to have an affair, although it will be nothing serious in the eyes of the other party as well as in yours, and you will have some money trouble on that account. There is a possibility of pregnancy. But you will do well if you are thinking of legal marriage. If you proceed in good order, you will have a happy home.

Like Fu-Sui-Kan (No. 38), this combination also promises luck in overseas propositions, and it suggests travel by air. Climbing step by step, you will eventually go a long way, though it will take time.

GENERAL: You will be lucky, but you have to make the right start if you want to maximize your luck. You are likely to move or be transferred, and whether you go north or south will considerably affect your future. In any case, follow the advice of your seniors and superiors.

FU-CHI-KAN

WISHES: It will be realized gradually.

MARRIAGE: It will be a good match.

BIRTH: A girl will be born safe.

HEALTH: Belated action may lead to death. Change doctors.

NEGOTIATIONS, DISPUTES: Slow progress will be to your advantage. Don't hurry.

TRAVELING: It will be a good trip. Possibly you will travel by air.

MISSING PROPERTY: Will not be found.

AWAITED PERSONS, MESSAGES: Coming late, with good news.

MONEY: You will have increasing luck with money.

MARKET: Generally balanced, with bearish overtones.

INDEX VARIATIONS:

1st place:	Fu-Ka-Ka-Jin	...... ○○●○●○
2nd place:	Son-I-Fu	.... ○○●○○●
3rd place:	Fu-Chi-Kan	.... ○○●●●●
4th place:	Ten-Zan-Ton	...... ○○○○●●
5th place:	Gon-I-Zan	.... ○●●○●●
6th place:	Sui-Zan-Ken	.... ●○●○●●

40. Fu-Chi-Kan ○○● ●●● Look at Yourself.

BOOK OF CHANGES: A gust of wind blows up a lot of dust. Beware of unwelcome surprises.

COMMENTS: This combination symbolizes August. Currently you seem to be involved in a mess and are having a hard time. But if you proceed with honesty and kindness, you will be rewarded by unexpected assistance. You are advised to look with an unbiased eye at things around you, and at yourself. Don't act blindly as others do. Insight based on careful analysis will make your position secure. As the combination also suggests teaching from above and obedience below, it promises much luck for educators and people in leading positions.

Change is another basic trend underlying your status. You may move to a new residence, or switch to a new job. Watch out for thieves and amorous temptors.

If you are a woman, you are probably beautiful, but your ideals may be too high. You're probably a perfectionist. You may be bothered by the difference between what you wish in your heart and what you see in reality. Whoever asks your hand, remember it is an opportunity. Aiming too high will get you nowhere. Happiness is within your reach if you just recognize it.

GENERAL: You will start well and end up not so well. But honesty and kindness will bring you more luck, possibly in the form of assistance from someone.

WISHES: It will come true, but not immediately as you wish.

MARRIAGE: You will marry if she (he) asks you, but not if you ask her (him).

BIRTH: There will be trouble.

HEALTH: Watch out for accidents.

NEGOTIATIONS, DISPUTES: You will lose if you hurry. Currently the other party is at an advantage.

TRAVELING: Don't get hurt due to carelessness.

MISSING PROPERTY: Will not be recovered.

AWAITED PERSONS, MESSAGES: A woman is making trouble. He (she) is wondering what to do.

MONEY: You will not be very well off.

MARKET: A sharp fall.

SUI-TEN-JU

INDEX VARIATIONS:

1st place:	Fu-Rai-Eki	........○○●●●○
2nd place:	Fu-Sui-Kan	........○○●●○●
3rd place:	Fu-Zan-Zen	........○○●○●●
4th place:	Ten-Chi-Hi	........○○○●●●
5th place:	San-Chi-Haku	......○●●●●●
6th place:	Sui-Chi-Hi	.........●○●●●●

"Water" ●○● Combinations

41. Sui-Ten-Ju

●○● ○○○ Not Now.

BOOK OF CHANGES: Wait, and save energy for to-morrow.

COMMENTS: As flower buds of a Japanese plum tree grow under snow, your fortune is improving potentially, though it will be some time before it blooms. When spring comes, the snow will melt, and there will be flowers everywhere. Currently your luck is on the rise but still premature. Perhaps you should relax and save energy for to-morrow. Impatience will bring you nothing but disaster. New plans will have little chance of success despite hard efforts, and if you try to fight your way through, you will be in trouble. Wait a little more, and someone will come and help you without your asking. Wait two months. If you have already spent a lot

SUI-TAKU-SETSU

of time on the proposition you have in mind, there may be a happy break even sooner. Whether you are a man or a woman, you are likely to have an affair with an older lover. Don't go too far in it, for you will have a hard time getting out of it.

GENERAL: Wait, and things will turn in your favor. Heaven blesses those who can wait. Just relax and save your energy. Soon a helping hand will be extended to you.

WISHES: It will be realized if you approach it gradually.

MARRIAGE: The proposition is premature. You will be sorry if you marry right now.

NEGOTIATIONS, DISPUTES: Be patient. Be persistent.

TRAVELING: Watch out for thieves and fires.

MISSING PROPERTY: It will be no use looking for it.

AWAITED PERSONS, MESSAGES: Coming late.

MONEY: You will have more luck with money, though not immediately. You will get an unexpected income.

MARKET: Bearish.

INDEX VARIATIONS:

1st place:	Sui-Fu-Sei	●○●○○●
2nd place:	Sui-Ka-Ki-Sai	●○●○●○
3rd place:	Sui-Taku-Setsu	●○●●○○
4th place:	Taku-Ten-Kai	●○○○○○
5th place:	Chi-Ten-Tai	●●●○○○
6th place:	Fu-Ten-Sho-Chiku	○○●○○○

42. Sui-Taku-Setsu ●○● ●○○ Exercise Moderation.

BOOK OF CHANGES: A fox in the mud is your symbol. You are unable to move fast, and you have a lot of dangerous temptations.

COMMENTS: You will not be unlucky if you stop whenever necessary, and proceed slowly and carefully. If you move hastily, you will simply bog down. Also, try to save, though you should not be stingy. Joys and sorrows will come to you alternately. Don't be excited too much if a happy development occurs. Be on the lookout for an unfavorable turn of events that might follow.

You will spend much in connection with your business, and an act of kindness may result in offending others. Temptations will be many. If anyone makes a seemingly attractive proposition to you, stop and think instead of jumping at it. Study the proposer carefully. Since the signal is amber, move slowly with caution.

If you are a woman, you may be deceived by someone you try to deceive. The other party is smarter than you.

GENERAL: Gains and setbacks will come to you in turn. Be temperate and moderate. You will become luckier by and by. Perhaps you tend to be too argumentative lately. You may find yourself in a fix on that account. And you may be slandered by others.

WISHES: A wish commensurate with your status will be granted.

MARRIAGE: You will marry. But you will fail if you hurry.

BIRTH: The baby will be born without much trouble, though with a little delay.

HEALTH: You may fall ill due to intemperance, either dietary or sexual. Other troubles are also possible.

NEGOTIATIONS, DISPUTES: You will fail if you use an intermediary. Your stand may be right, but you are at a disadvantage nevertheless.

TRAVELING: You are likely to have some trouble on the

SUI-KA-KI-SAI

trip. Your itinerary will be disturbed. The best thing is not to go.

MISSING PROPERTY: It will not be found immediately, but a long time later you will realize where it has been all the time.

AWAITED PERSONS, MESSAGES: Coming very late.

MONEY: Your income will be irregular. Save and provide for your next major move. You will have to pay high interest on loans.

MARKET: Generally unchanged with bearish undercurrents.

INDEX VARIATIONS:

    1st place: Kan-I-Sui .... ●○●●○●
    2nd place: Sui-Rai-Chun ...... ●○●●●○
    3rd place: Sui-Ten-Ju .... ●○●○○○
    4th place: Dai-I-Taku.......... ●○○●○○
    5th place: Chi-Taku-Rin ...... ●●●●○○
    6th place: Fu-Taku-Chu-Bu .... ○○●●○○

43. Sui-Ka-Ki-Sai ●○● ○●○ Established in Fame.

BOOK OF CHANGES: In a state ideally balanced and ordered, all things are in fulfillment.

COMMENTS: Now that everything has been done, the only thing you can do is to preserve what has been accomplished. The joy of fulfillment is followed by a sense of dreariness. You miss something, as after making love.

Your fortune is favorable for the moment, but may decline somewhat as you go on. You had better provide against what is forthcoming. Following old ways will bring you more luck than starting new things. You may feel that something is going wrong in your relations with the person you have in mind—a senior, a friend, or your lover. Try to make up through an intermediary.

The wish now in your heart will come true temporarily, but what you have obtained may be lost again if you ask too much. Moderation is important in seeking any objective. Avoid carelessness and negligence if you want to stay lucky.

If you are expecting to marry, you will have success so far as the wedding itself is concerned, but you may have trouble later. If you are married, slight disharmony underlies what appears to be a peaceful home life, with supressed desires lurking in the heart of either husband or wife. There may be unpleasant discoveries, such as a secret affair between the husband and the housemaid. Between unmarried lovers, too, there may be similar disturbing revelations related to sex.

This combination suggests sexual excesses. Avoid overexertion.

GENERAL: There will be frequent ups and downs in your luck. For better results, proceed in cooperation or in consultation with others. You tend to flirt a lot.

WISHES: It will be delayed due to a little trouble.

MARRIAGE: You will marry him (her), but you will be dissatisfied later. Make thorough investigations now.

BIRTH: Safe.

HEALTH: A seemingly slight ailment may linger. Beware of sexual neurasthenia.

NEGOTIATIONS, DISPUTES: You may be verging on a catastrophe. Be humble.

TRAVELING: You will have a problem possibly one related to sex.

SUI-RAI-CHUN

MISSING PROPERTY: It will be no use looking for it for the moment.

AWAITED PERSONS, MESSAGES: Coming. But the reply will be the opposite of what you are wishing.

MONEY: You will fail if you hurry.

MARKET: Down.

INDEX VARIATIONS:

1st place:	Sui-Zan-Ken	●○●○●●
2nd place:	Sui-Ten-Ju	●○●○○○
3rd place:	Sui-Rai-Chun	●○●●●○
4th place:	Taku-Ka-Kaku	●○○○●○
5th place:	Chi-Ka-Mei-I	●●●○●○
6th place:	Fu-Ka-Ka-Jin	○○●○●○

44. Sui-Rai-Chun ●○● ●●○ Growth in Check.

BOOK OF CHANGES: The dragon stays low in the water, unable to raise its head. This is one of the four worst combinations in Yi augury.

COMMENTS: Frankly, your fortune is not favorable. You are in trouble and unable to grow. Despite your wish to move on with hope, circumstances simply don't permit you to do so. Marriage proposals will not amount to anything, at least for the time being. You are, as it were, a seed in the ground, trying to shoot up its bud with tremendous effort, although the ground is still frozen hard. It will take all your energy to break it, and if you overstrain yourself in impatience, you may perish before you can see the light of day.

So, remember that your luck is down right now. Take unpleasant developments and losses with a brave heart, and persevere until the time comes for you to start up. Wait at least three months.

Since your index variation will tell you how soon such a change for the better will arrive, find your index number and carefully consider where you stand. The combination has affinity to the number "4." Perhaps you will have a happy break in four months.

You will have many problems with respect to your job, residence, and monetary affairs. If you need advice or help, you had better turn to inferiors and women rather than to elders or superiors. Yi augury does not always tell you to consult people above yourself.

GENERAL: Your intentions may be right but your circumstances do not permit you to carry them out. Be patient and mark time.

WISHES: New wishes will not be realized immediately, but there is no reason why you shouldn't sow the seed now. You will have more luck later on. Keep trying.

MARRIAGE: After a delay, you will eventually marry. The number "4" will have a lot to do with the match.

BIRTH: A boy will be born after much labor.

HEALTH: Beware of a nervous breakdown, hysteria, poor looks due to constipation.

NEGOTIATIONS, DISPUTES: No immediate settlement is forthcoming. Have an agent take over.

TRAVELING: Cancel the trip. There will be troubles related to water or sex if you go.

MISSING PROPERTY: It will be hard to find.

AWAITED PERSONS, MESSAGES: Coming late.

MONEY: You will have money problems. Ask a woman or an inferior for a loan.

MARKET: An upward trend will be held in check until a

SUI-FU-SEI

minor break occurs in four days or four weeks, although the general level will stay unchanged. Refrain from action for the moment.

INDEX VARIATIONS:

1st place:	Sui-Chi-Hi	●○●●●●
2nd place:	Sui-Taku-Setsu	●○●●○○
3rd place:	Sui-Ka-Ki-Sai	●○●○●○
4th place:	Taku-Rai-Zui	●○○●●○
5th place:	Chi-Rai-Fuku	●●●●●○
6th place:	Fu-Rai-Eki	○○●●●○

45. Sui-Fu-Sei ●○● ○○● Back and Forth.

BOOK OF CHANGES: You will move up and down, like a pail used to draw water from a well. But all this movement is not useless. You are drawing water.

COMMENTS: Don't row against the stream, and refrain from effecting changes or entering anything new. Instead of seeking novelties, concentrate on what you are doing, and stay where you are. Soon a helping hand will be extended from above.

You may be tempted to change your plans or switch to a new job or business, but you should do no such thing. You will not merely be unsuccessful, but also fall into the well and drown.

Frankly, your fortune is not favorable, but the situation is not so gloomy as Kan-I-Sui (No. 46) or Taku-Sui-Kon (No. 14). You are advised to relax and save energy instead of putting up a useless fight against your destiny. Don't do anything rash. Stay just where you are.

This combination suggests the status of a virtuous person benefiting others with noble acts. This means that you are an individual of caliber, who even in adversity is counted on by others for help and advice. Do whatever you can for them. Good deeds always pay off.

Whether you are a man or a woman, and whether you are married or unmarried, a break seems almost coming, but you will not separate as you move back and forth. Perhaps the physical bond is too strong.

GENERAL: Mistakes and misunderstandings will occur frequently, giving you much trouble.

WISHES: A small wish will be granted. Big ones will not.

MARRIAGE: You will make smooth progress at first, but eventually the proposition will be called off.

BIRTH: There will be much trouble.

HEALTH: There is much possibility of a relapse, and once it occurs there will be little chance of complete recovery. Sexual indulgence may be the cause.

NEGOTIATIONS, DISPUTES: There may be a last-minute turn for the worse. Be humble and persistent.

TRAVELING: Cancel the trip.

MISSING PROPERTY: It is in the house.

AWAITED PERSONS, MESSAGES: Not coming for some reason.

MONEY: Money will come and go smoothly. You will be fairly lucky with money. You will be able to get loans.

MARKET: There will be ups and downs, followed by an eventual fall.

INDEX VARIATIONS:

1st place:	Sui-Ten-Ju	●○●○○○
2nd place:	Sui-Zan-Ken	●○●○●●
3rd place:	Kan-I-Sui	●○●●○●
4th place:	Taku-Fu-Tai-Ka	●○○○○●
5th place:	Chi-Fu-Sho	●●●○○●
6th place:	Son-I-Fu	○○●○○●

KAN-I-SUI

46. Kan-I-Sui ●○● ●○● In a Fix.

BOOK OF CHANGES: Both helper and
helped are drowning. Of the four
worst combinations in Yi augury,
this foretells a fall.

COMMENTS: Ladened with valuable
cargo, your boat has capsized in a
storm. Your struggling feet naturally
cannot touch the bottom, and your friend, who has
tried to help you, is now drowning with you. The situation is almost desperate.

Though in a terrible fix, you can hope to survive
the crisis by acting bravely with a cool head, re-
cognizing that you are at the bottom of your cycle
of fortunes, and refraining from rash acts to minimize
your loss until the next surge of luck helps you out
of the present mess.

If your company or family has split into two hostile
groups, take best care not to be involved in the feud.
You have enough trouble without it, and petty tricks
will merely increase your difficulty. In an internal
conflict both you and your opponents are likely to be
punished, and since the combination suggests trouble
about your residence, you might be transferred to some
remote place or compelled to leave home.

Heavy losses or considerable inconveniences may befall you due to joint undertakings with others or on
account of others' faults. Watch out for swindlers and
thieves.

On emotional matters, your heart may sustain a
wound that will leave a life-long scar.

Many women drawing this combination are those

burdened with permanent family problems or sad experiences in the past. Some are in the gay trade, drifting from one place to another, and falling.

There is a possibility of a double suicide. In any case, find your index number and consult your index variation to see how soon you will have a break in this bad spell. Since you are at the bottom now, you are bound to move up sooner or later if you persevere. Be courageous.

The combination, however, means good luck to religious or academic people, promising them relief from troubles and leadership in their respective fields.

GENERAL: You probably feel you are out of condition physically. You will experience a lot of difficulties with respect to sex and other phases of your physical life. And you will be unlucky with money. In short, you are in the worst state. There is no use trying to find a way out. Instead, just wait until the bad spell comes to an end. There will be a change for the better in two or five months, and then things will improve gradually. If you had today or this week in mind when you got this combinations, watch out for fevers, criminal troubles, and traffic accidents. You are in danger.

WISHES: It will not come true.

MARRIAGE: It will be safe not to accept any proposal right now.

BIRTH: You will have twins, or possibly a miscarriage.

HEALTH: Beware of neurosis, brain diseases, and fevers. You may be in a dangerous condition temporarily.

NEGOTIATIONS, DISPUTES: Both sides will lose after wasting much time.

SUI-ZAN-KEN

TRAVELING: Beware of disaster by water, and theft.

MISSING PROPERTY: If stolen, it will not be recovered. If you left it somewhere, it is in a pretty place but will not be found immediately.

AWAITED PERSONS, MESSAGES: Not coming due to disturbance.

MONEY: You will be hard up. No loans will be obtained for the moment.

MARKET: A debacle will occur.

INDEX VARIATIONS:

1st place:	Sui-Taku-Setsu	●○●○○
2nd place:	Sui-Chi-Hi	●○●●●
3rd place:	Sui-Fu-Sei	●○●○○●
4th place:	Taku-Sui-Kon	●○○●○●
5th place:	Chi-Sui-Shi	●●●○●
6th place:	Fu-Sui-Kan	○○●●○●

47. Sui-Zan-Ken

●○● ○●● Complications On All Sides.

BOOK OF CHANGES: The dragon has lost the jewel in its palm. You are likely to lose a fortune, or something very precious to you. This is one of the four worst combinations in Yi augury.

COMMENTS: You are lame and helpless in a terrible fix, surrounded by all sorts of difficulties and problems. Faced with one misfortune after another, you really don't know what to do. If you try to push ahead, you will find the path getting narrower as you go. Capable as you are, every move you make invariably works against your purpose, and the harder you struggle, the deeper you bog down. Your relations with the opposite sex will be hopelessly complicated, making it impossible for you to take any effective action. You are in danger of ruining yourself and losing all you have. Be careful not to be swindled or tricked. You will have trouble with your residence, and you may be robbed. Against this spell of misfortunes, what can you do? There is only one thing you can do: face the fact that you are currently out of Fortune's favor, and stay where you are, doing nothing. Just persevere. Concentrate on your usual work and wait until the storm passes. If possible, try to read at your leisure. Good books will give you much food for thought, enabling you to learn more about life. As the combination also foretells a helping hand from considerate people, you may look forward to assistance from your seniors and superiors for a little while. With the help of good advisors, you will be able to get along.

GENERAL: Everything you do will produce disappointing results. You are, as it were, trying to run on crutches. You cannot expect to go very fast, and if you hurry, you will just stumble. It would be much better if you rest awhile and save energy. Perhaps you will get useful advice from your superiors.

WISHES: It will not be realized easily, though there will be more chance of realization if it is a modest wish.

MARRIAGE: The proposition sounds attractive but is not very favorable actually. You had better call it off.

BIRTH: There will be a little trouble, and the baby may be sickly.

HEALTH: You may become seriously ill. Beware of trou-

SUI-CHI-HI

bles and accidents that will affect your lower limbs.

NEGOTIATIONS, DISPUTES: You will make slow progress. If you are in a dispute, seek a private settlement.

TRAVELING: There will be trouble on the way.

MISSING PROPERTY: It was stolen, or it has been lost among other things and will not be found.

AWAITED PERSONS, MESSAGES: Not coming immediately. He (she) is in trouble.

MONEY: You will be rather hard up. Loans will be difficult to obtain unless they are small.

MARKET: Down.

INDEX VARIATIONS:

1st place:	Sui-Ka-Ki-Sai	●○●○●○
2nd place:	Sui-Fu-Sei	●○●○○●
3rd place:	Sui-Chi-Hi	●○●●●●
4th place:	Taku-Zan-Kan	●○○○●●
5th place:	Chi-Zan-Ken	●●●○●●
6th place:	Fu-Zan-Zen	○○●○●●

48. Sui-Chi-Hi ●○● ●●●
Busy Days.

BOOK OF CHANGES: Impressive constellations revolve around the North Star. After a big war, peace has returned at last, but there are hard post-war problems yet to be solved. Though the crisis is over, well-considered wise action is required to bring your work to final glory.

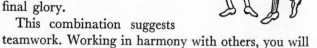

This combination suggests teamwork. Working in harmony with others, you will be successful, especially in joint undertakings with close associates. In any case, choose a good partner, and observe etiquette in dealing with him (her) without becoming excessively familiar to the point of being rude. Mutual respect is vital between lovers, between teacher and pupils, between parents and children, between brothers and sisters, and between man and wife. Familiarity often results in impolite words and acts, which in turn breed hidden antipathy, mistrust, and contempt in the hearts of others.

You are advised to follow a righteous man going a righteous way if you want to proceed smoothly and happily. If you accept wise advice and suggestions from your friends and superiors, they will help you in return, and you will be doing well at all times. So far as teamwork is maintained, move aggressively; and once you have taken action, work hard to lead all others in performance.

If you are expecting to marry, you can look forward to a happy, harmonious home life.

GENERAL: Turn to your superiors and friends for good advice, and follow their suggestions if you want to be better off. You will be successful in any joing undertaking.

WISHES: It will come true.

MARRIAGE: It will be a good match. But it may be called off if you hesitate.

BIRTH: A girl will be born safe.

HEALTH: If you are ill, you cannot expect quick recovery. Beware of skin diseases.

NEGOTIATIONS, DISPUTES: You will do well with the assistance of a friend or friends.

SAN-TEN-TAI-CHIKU

TRAVELING: A vacation trip is commendable.

MISSING PROPERTY: It will be found if you look for it at once. With more time lost, it will be harder to recover.

AWAITED PERSONS, MESSAGES: You will hear from him (her).

MONEY: Speculation or gambling will produce fatal results.

MARKET: A bearish, unchanged state will be followed by a decline.

INDEX VARIATIONS:

1st place:	Sui-Rai-Chun	●○●●●○
2nd place:	Kan-I-Sui	●○●●○●
3rd place:	Sui-Zan-Ken	●○○●○●
4th place:	Taku-Chi-Sui	●○○●●●
5th place:	Kon-I-Chi	●●●●○●
6th place:	Fu-Chi-Kan	○○●●●●

"Mountain" ○●● Combinations

49. San-Ten-Tai-Chiku ○●● ○○○ Mark Time.

BOOK OF CHANGES: A dragon in the mountain is struggling impatiently to ascend to Heaven. After a temporary impasse, a radical turn for the better will occur. Your luck is strongly on the rise.

COMMENTS: A dragon in an agonizing effort to start skyward before it's time is your symbol. With an unsatisfied desire, you are probably in an unstable, irritable state of mind. But despite all your impatience, the time has not arrived yet for you to start, and forcible action and overstraining will serve no purpose. Instead, you are advised to improve your mind and enlarge your faculties at this opportunity.

Being a dragon, you have enough caliber to rise to Heaven some day. Instead of being irritated and frustrated, you should save your energy and improve yourself until you have the next surge of good luck. The combination promises you a happy turn of events after a temporary impasse. You can look forward to stability and growth on a new plane.

If you are a woman, you may not be an exceeding beauty of the conventional type, but you are probably healthy and aggressive, and a little self-willed, but certainly very intelligent. Try to be less self-assertive, and softer and sweeter. If you do, you will be more popular, and in six months or so a worthy man will ask your hand.

GENERAL: Through many difficulties, you will eventually achieve your goal. If you are not frustrated halfway through, you will get all desired results. You may have a wrangle with a close friend. This time you should yield.

WISHES: It will take much time, but will be realized eventually if you are not aiming too high.

MARRIAGE: Don't hurry if you want to avoid future complications. Relax and wait for an approach from the other party for better results.

BIRTH: A boy will be born safe, though with a little delay.

HEALTH: You are in delicate physical condition due to overstraining. You may have spots and erruptions on

SAN-TAKU-SON

your skin. Constipation may be the cause. Sleep well, and eat fresh vegetables.

NEGOTIATIONS, DISPUTES: You will have to wait a long time until the other party calls for a settlement.

TRAVELING: You may have an accident on the trip, and there may be trouble at home while you are away.

MISSING PROPERTY: It is in the northeast. Look for it patiently.

AWAITED PERSONS, MESSAGES: There will be much delay. The combination foretells considerable obstruction.

MONEY: You will be lucky with money, and you can expect to get loans.

MARKET: Up. There will be a departure from the balanced state pretty soon, but short buying or selling is inadvisable. Long-term operations will be profitable.

INDEX VARIATIONS:

1st place:	San-Pu-Ko	○●●○○●
2nd place:	San-Ka-Hi	○●●○●○
3rd place:	San-Taku-Son	○●●●○○
4th place:	Ka-Ten-Tai-Yu	○●○○○○
5th place:	Fu-Ten-Sho-Chiku ..	○○●○○○
6th place:	Chi-Ten-Tai	●●●○○○

50. San-Taku-Son

○●● ●○○ Give Freely.

BOOK OF CHANGES: Unselfish service will cost you much immediately but pay off handsomely later.

COMMENTS: You will suffer temporary losses, in the pecuniary way or otherwise, but you will later have material gains or be honored on that account.

Free service pays well these days. Whatever benefit you give to other people will pay you dividends worth many times your original investment. Your present losses are not total losses. If you are going angling, the combination promises you best luck, and it foretells ideal happiness if you are expecting to marry. Though there is a little tendency to feminine predominance, there will be harmony between man and wife, and you will have nice children. With peace at home, the husband will go a long way in his career. But if you indulge in your happiness too much, you may incur the jealousy of others. If you are a woman, you may tend to talk excessively.

If you are aiming to get a contract, you will succeed after awhile. But remember, greed will result in heavy losses. Avoid gambling. If you want to maximize your gains, be unselfish.

GENERAL: Emphasis on spiritual matters will bring you luck. Only temporary gains will be obtained through any attempt to utilize others for your own purposes. Benefiting others will do good to yourself as well as to the benefited. New plans and new investments are advisable. They will pay.

WISHES: It will be realized seventy to eighty percent.

MARRIAGE: It is a good match, but don't hurry.

BIRTH: Very safe.

HEALTH: There is a tendency to excessive mutual service, and you are both tired. Surely it is good to satisfy her (him), but don't overdo it.

SAN-KA-HI

NEGOTIATIONS, DISPUTES: Ask a trusted superior or friend for help. Don't try to do it alone.

TRAVELING: There will be a little trouble, and your return home will be delayed.

MISSING PROPERTY: Will not be found immediately.

AWAITED PERSONS, MESSAGES: He (she) will come if you call, not once but several times.

MONEY: A seeming loss will later turn out to be a substantial gain. You will earn more than you spend.

MARKET: A slow fall due to much selling will be followed by an upturn.

INDEX VARIATIONS:

1st place:	San-Sui-Mo	○●●●○●
2nd place:	San-Rai-I	○●●●●○
3rd place:	San-Ten-Tai-Chiku	○●●○○○
4th place:	Ka-Taku-Kei	○●○●○○
5th place:	Fu-Taku-Chu-Bu	○○●●○○
6th place:	Chi-Taku-Rin	●●●●○○

51. San-Ka-Hi ○●● ○●○ In the Limelight.

BOOK OF CHANGES: Whatever the pretenses, you are you —nothing more, nothing less.

COMMENTS: Sincerity seldom lies behind sweet words, as the Chinese saying goes. But people are apt to be dazed by glamorous appearances, not realizing the emptiness they cover so cleverly. You are in danger of being cheated. If anyone approaches you with an alluring proposal, watch out. You will be successful on small matters, but big plans and undertakings will be risky unless you have enough foresight. Make thorough investigations beforehand. Also, you may have a break with an old friend or associate. In a dispute or conflict, bluffs and pretenses will help you but little. The sooner you give up, the better.

If you are expecting to marry, you are likely to be disappointed. The match-maker's story may be unreliable. Or you may be disillusioned with each other, you being a showy type and the other party being conservative. Remember that the present combination foretells defeated expectations. However, it also implies success based on extensive popularity. In art, entertainment, broadcasting, and other glamorous fields, you will have a good chance of carrying out your plans or ideas successfully as showiness agrees with your present state. You may proceed with confidence, and you will find good assistants. Perhaps you may have something to do with night-club hostesses or show-girls.

GENERAL: You are rather hard up as you tend to spend more than you earn. You should cut your spending. But if you are in a showy field like art, entertainment, or broadcasting, such free spending may help you later in your career.

WISHES: It will be realized with a little delay.

MARRIAGE: The proposition will come to nothing in the end. Since you have much chance of being disillusioned, you had better not accept any proposal at the present moment—not merely on marriage, but also in negotiations, business, employment, etc.

BIRTH: A girl will be born safe.

HEALTH: A fever may become serious.

NEGOTIATIONS, DISPUTES: Use an intermediary for better results.

TRAVELING: You will be lucky on any trip.

SAN-RAI-I

MISSING PROPERTY: It will be hard to find.

AWAITED PERSONS, MESSAGES: Coming late.

MONEY: You will be hard up internally. A little money may be borrowed.

MARKET: Despite a seemingly bullish trend, the general level will be rather low.

INDEX VARIATIONS:

1st place:	Gon-I-Zan	○●●○●●
2nd place:	San-Ten-Tai-Chiku	○●●○○○
3rd place:	San-Rai-I	○●●●●○
4th place:	Ri-I-Ka	○●○○●○
5th place:	Fu-Ka-Ka-Jin	○○●○●○
6th place:	Chi-Ka-Mei-I	●●●○●○

52. San-Rai-I ○●● ●●○ The "Mouth" Problem.

BOOK OF CHANGES: The combination symbolizes the mouth, the upper jaw being stationary while the lower jaw moves up and down. You have many mouths to feed, and problems will occur about them—not merely your own family but also others related to you.

COMMMENTS: The mouth can be the source of many problems with respect to its two functions, eating and talking. Careless words will do you a lot of harm, and so will intemperance in eating and drinking. Despite its peaceful appearance, the situation you are in is fraught with dangers. In a dispute or a love affair, especially, you should act carefully, exercising moderation and waiting patiently until the trouble, whatever it is, comes to an end. A slip of the tongue or an innocent lie may produce serious consequences, and you will have a hard time explaining yourself. On your job, you may find yourself in an awkward position, sandwiched between an adamant supervisor and demanding subordinates. All this will make you very uncomfortable, but unfortunately all you can do at the present moment is to continue to perform your duties without complaining. And consult your index variation. You will not have much chance of doing better if your index number is 1 or 3, but otherwise you can look forward to a favorable break in the near future.

You are advised to take good care of yourself, particularly your teeth, stomach and other digestive organs.

GENERAL: The fruit of your labor may be lost because of someone else. Your superiors and subordinates will not help. You should look for a sympathetic helper among your friends or co-workers. If you are jobless right now, you will soon be able to feed many mouths including yours.

WISHES: It will be realized, but the results will be a little different from what you are expecting now.

MARRIAGE: You will marry the person of your choice, but financial difficulties will follow, unless both of you are prepared to work.

HEALTH: Be careful of what you eat. Your stomach and liver are failing.

NEGOTIATIONS, DISPUTES: It will drag on. No settlement will be made unless you compromise.

TRAVELING: You may go on the trip unless it is very long.

MISSING PROPERTY: Look in the closet. Outside your home, look northeast.

AWAITED PERSONS, MESSAGES: He (she) is likely to be very late. Someone is stopping him (her).

MONEY: You will get enough money to live on.

MARKET: Unchanged.

SAN-PU-KO

INDEX VARIATIONS:

1st place: San-Chi-Haku ......○●●●●●
2nd place: San-Taku-Son ......○●●●○○
3rd place: San-Ka-Hi ....○●●○●○
4th place: Ka-Rai-Zei-Go ......○●○●●○
5th place: Fu-Rai-Eki ....○○●●●○
6th place: Chi-Rai-Fuku........●●●●●○

53. San-Pu-Ko

○●● ○○● Cut Out the Cancer.

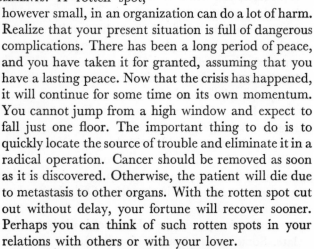

BOOK OF CHANGES: A thief is inside the gate, threatening the security of the entire household.

COMMENTS: A rotten spot, however small, in an organization can do a lot of harm. Realize that your present situation is full of dangerous complications. There has been a long period of peace, and you have taken it for granted, assuming that you have a lasting peace. Now that the crisis has happened, it will continue for some time on its own momentum. You cannot jump from a high window and expect to fall just one floor. The important thing to do is to quickly locate the source of trouble and eliminate it in a radical operation. Cancer should be removed as soon as it is discovered. Otherwise, the patient will die due to metastasis to other organs. With the rotten spot cut out without delay, your fortune will recover sooner. Perhaps you can think of such rotten spots in your relations with others or with your lover.

Do your best to improve the deteriorating situation.

Overcome your own weaknesses and faults to make the best of your future opportunities. You will receive pressure from others, or witness disharmony in your own family, or have trouble with your parents or children. But impatience at this moment will merely make matters worse. Consult your index variation to see how soon a change for the better is forthcoming, and wait patiently until the time comes.

If you are a woman, you are probably suffering from complicated love problems. Even if you are unmarried, the chances are that you have gone fairly far in the affair. If you are a widow, a young lover may cause disturbance in your home. There is a possibility of illicit conception.

GENERAL: Your luck is on the decline, with a rupture or break threatening. You are apt to take eccentric action that will surprise others.

WISHES: It will not be realized due to internal disturbance.

MARRIAGE: He (she) is in love with someone else.

BIRTH: Beware of miscarriage.

HEALTH: Undergo close examinations. Depending on their results, an operation may be necessary.

NEGOTIATIONS, DISPUTES: It will drag on.

TRAVELING: Watch out for thieves.

MISSING PROPERTY: Look east or north.

Awaited persons, messages: Not coming due to interference from a woman.

MONEY: Your balance will be in the red due to much internal spending.

MARKET: A slow fall will be followed by a sharp rise.

INDEX VARIATIONS:

1st place: San-Ten-Tai-Chiku .. ○●●○○○
  2nd place: Gon-I-Zan .... ○●●●○●●
  3rd place: San-Sui-Mo .... ○●●●●○●
  4th place: Ka-Fu-Tei .... ○●○○○●
  5th place: Son-I-Fu .... ○○●○○●
  6th place: Chi-Fu-Sho.......... ●●●○○●

54. San-Sui-Mo ○●● ●○● Veiled in a Mist.

BOOK OF CHANGES: A mist is obstructing your view at present, but soon it will clear up and you will be able to see more clearly.

Symbolic of enlightenment and education, this combination suggests a bright future for a child.

COMMENTS: It takes a lot of effort and patience to educate children, but much can be expected of their future.

As in education, rash action is most inadvisable in whatever you are doing. Though you may be in an uneasy, unstable state of mind, don't make snap decisions on your own judgment.

Always talk to a senior or a superior first if you want to be successful.

You may not have much luck at present, but you will be increasingly luckier as you go on. So cheer up.

This combination is a sign of good luck for children, young hopefuls, new undertakings, and other things envisaging future growth. Also, you will be go very far in academic pursuit or research.

You had better not think of marriage right now. Both you and your prospective spouse will be disappointed, and the relationship between you two may become a vague, informal one. However, a woman in a gay trade looking for a "patron" will have much success if she gets this combination.

GENERAL: You tend to run to extremes in a hurry. Following a senior's advice, turn about. Your luck will then be on the rise again.

WISHES: Wish just one thing, and it will be granted if it is commensurate with your status. You will have no success if you hurry, or if you ask too much.

MARRIAGE: You will not marry him (her).

BIRTH: Reasonably safe.

HEALTH: Beware of troubles affecting your digestive organs. The ailment will linger a little.

NEGOTIATIONS, DISPUTES: You are still at a disadvantage.

TRAVELING: Cancel the trip. You will be robbed or fall ill if you go.

MISSING PROPERTY: It will not be found. Perhaps it will help to ask children.

Awaited persons, messages: He (she) intends to come but will be late.

MONEY: You are likely to have trouble about a bill or a bond. Loans will be hard to obtain.

MARKET: Generally unchanged with bearish undercurrents.

INDEX VARIATIONS:

1st place:	San-Taku-Son	○●●●○○
2nd place:	San-Chi-Haku	○●●●●●
3rd place:	San-Pu-Ko	○●●○○●
4th place:	Ka-Sui-Bi-Sai	○●○●○●
5th place:	Fu-Sui-Kan	○○●●○●
6th place:	Chi-Sui-Shi	●●●●○●

GON-I-ZAN

55. Gon-I-Zan ○●● ○●● Rock-
   climbing.

BOOK OF CHANGES: The gate in a
   mountain pass has been closed,
   barring your progress.

COMMENTS: With a barrier standing
   in your way, you are now mark-
   ing time, unable to proceed further. As in rock climbing, an impatient move at this moment will
   be most dangerous. You will be
   risking your life that way.

Currently, circumstances forbid you from venturing
forward. You have to learn to stop when you should,
and start again when you can. Continue whatever you
have been doing, but don't begin anything new. The
same applies to your marriage prospects.

As the combination symbolizes the meeting point
of two adjacent mountains—fortune and misfortune—
you may find yourself in a mixture of good and bad
luck. For instance, you may be doing well on your job
while you are rather short of money. In business, you
will have difficulty in finding a good partner.

You are advised to remain steady, solid and im-
movable like a mountain, taking as little action as
possible and carefully watching the situation so that
you can move fast at the first sign of your recovering
luck. Be practical instead of proud.

GENERAL: You are now irritable and glum, what with
   pressure from superiors and hindered progress in your
   plans. Your nerves are frayed.

SAN-CHI-HAKU

Perhaps you should go to a place of worship and meditate. In any case, realize that you should not, and cannot, move forward for the time being.

WISHES: It seems almost coming true but will not be realized easily because of many hindrances.

MARRIAGE: You will have many proposals, but none of them will mean much.

BIRTH: There will be a delay.

HEALTH: Your illness will not be cured quickly. Beware of neuralgia, rheumatism, and liver trouble.

NEGOTIATIONS, DISPUTES: Talk with patience and without hurry for better results.

TRAVELING: You will end up canceling the trip.

MISSING PROPERTY: It is in the house.

AWAITED PERSONS, MESSAGES: Not coming.

MONEY: Take care to avoid costly mistakes. Loans may be obtained after repeated efforts.

MARKET: Generally balanced. Don't buy or sell after getting this combination. You will lose.

INDEX VARIATIONS:

1st place:	San-Ka-Hi	○●●○●○
2nd place:	San-Pu-Ko	○●●○○●
3rd place:	San-Chi-Haku	○●●●●●
4th place:	Ka-Zan-Ryo	○●○○●●
5th place:	Fu-Zan-Zen	○○●○●●
6th place:	Chi-Zan-Ken	●●●○●●

56. San-Chi-Haku ○●● ●●●—Beware of Parasites.

BOOK OF CHANGES: Look at this combination. Having only one positive element against five negative, it shows little virility and spells a decline. But obtained at a moment when your luck is poorest, it tells you that a complete change from the old state is near at hand.

COMMENTS: A mountain gradually losing shape due to erosion is your symbol. Your luck is on the decline. Despite your high personal abilities and useful connections, you should not start anything new at this moment. Parasites among your colleagues and subordinates are looking for a chance to pull you down. Remember that the combination foretells a downfall. A minor development unfavorable to you, seemingly unimportant at first, may produce increasingly serious consequences and affect you fatally. Listen to the advice of your seniors and superiors.

As the combination also suggests internal emptiness, take care not to be deluded by impressive appearances, whether in business or in relations with other people.

The combination symbolizes September.

If you are a woman, the man approaching you with sweet words is most likely insincere. But since you seem to be strongly attracted to him, try to look at it this way: he represents the one positive element in this combination, dealing with five women at the same time. He is flirting with all of them, and possibly taking money from each. To convince yourself, have him investigated thoroughly. Don't go very far with him without knowing anything about him.

Now, another implication of this combination is a complete change from the worst state, a rebirth. An apparently dead tree may miraculously put out pretty flowers one spring. If you are having the worst luck at present, you may be sure that a happy break in the depressing spell is drawing near.

GENERAL: Stay on guard if you want to avoid a downfall. And watch out for thieves, fires, and traffic accidents.

WISHES: It will be realized gradually, but not immediately.

MARRIAGE: You will be unlucky if you are marrying for the first time, but you can look forward to happiness if it is going to be your second marriage.

BIRTH: Safe. But overstraining will lead to miscarriage.

HEALTH: Sexual enervation due to excesses and impotency due to alcoholism might befall you. If the patient is old and has been ill for some time, he needs the best care. Change doctors.

NEGOTIATIONS, DISPUTES: It will take time. You are handicapped by your lack of enthusiasm.

TRAVELING: You may have a little trouble on your way home. Don't travel by air.

MISSING PROPERTY: Will not be recovered.

AWAITED PERSONS, MESSAGES: Coming with much delay.

MONEY: You will lose much money on account of other people. But you will be moderately lucky with money if you don't ask too much. Be satisfied with about fifty percent of what you have in mind.

MARKET: Steadily down.

INDEX VARIATIONS:

1st place:	San-Rai-I	○●●●●○
2nd place:	San-Sui-Mo	○●●●○●
3rd place:	Gon-I-Zan	○●●○●●
4th place:	Ka-Chi-Shin	○●○●●●
5th place:	Fu-Chi-Kan	○○●●●●
6th place:	Kon-I-Chi	●●●●●●

CHI-TEN-TAI

"Earth" ●●● Combinations

57. Chi-Ten-Tai

●●● ○○○ Peace on Earth.

BOOK OF CHANGES: Without wind the lake is as placid as a mirror and everything is peaceful. Best luck is assured for those expecting to marry.

COMMENTS: Your luck is strongly on the rise. The combination symbolizes January, the beginning of a year. With its happy implications, it spells peace and success. You may look forward to smooth progress in company mergers, joint undertakings, marriages, theatrical productions, publications, etc. But just because everything goes so well, you may become too optimistic and careless, and indulgence and laziness may lead you to failure. As the popular saying goes, too much luck is close to bad luck. Though you are very lucky, you should always be on the lookout to avoid pitfalls. Your luck has much to do with the way you live. Except in turbulent eras, success usually comes from constant efforts continued patiently, and good luck must be coupled with general good performance to bring about happy results.

You will be favored by your superiors at your working place and enjoy well-rounded happiness at home. People with unhappy home situations almost never get this combination. You will have nice children. But you may have some problems in connection with your residence or in your relations with the opposite sex. If you are an office-girl, refrain from imprudent acts that may cause unfavorable talk about you, since you will marry before long.

Quite apart from all this, the combination also implies a sweet-tongued swindler or an over confident woman.

GENERAL: You are at the height of your luck, but after reaching the summit, the only way you can go is downward. Just because you are doing very well now, brace yourself up. The combination promises happiness and prosperity to virtuous, wise people but is too good for undeserving small men and women. You can count on your good luck unless you over-reach yourself.

WISHES: It will be granted. But don't hurry.

MARRIAGE: It will be a good match. Some fault-finders among prospective in-law, may raise objections, but you will end up marrying successfully.

BIRTH: Safe.

HEALTH: You may have a slight ailment due to intemperance, but it will be nothing serious.

NEGOTIATIONS, DISPUTES: You will fail if you go too far.

TRAVELING: You will travel with someone of the opposite sex. You are likely to spend much money.

MISSING PROPERTY: It will be found soon, but it may be broken.

AWAITED PERSONS, MESSAGES: Will come without fail if you call.

MONEY: You will be lucky with money, and loans will be obtained without difficulty. But imprudence may completely reverse the trend.

MARKET: Balanced at a favorable level.

CHI-TAKU-RIN

58. Chi-Taku-Rin ●●● ●○○ Timely Action.

BOOK OF CHANGES: The noble and the humble mix in harmony and friendship. Wishes commensurate with your status will be granted.

COMMENTS: The combination symbolizes December. As it spells progress, you will have success in whatever you seek in proper order if it is proportionate to your status, and you will be increasingly luckier. You will be dealing with many people, and will be engaged in two lines of business at the same time. Both will go well, but you will have many things to worry about. Since your luck is on the rise, you may take extemporaneous action by thinking quickly to adapt yourself to newly-developing circumstances. You tend to be capricious and dictatorial. You have to learn to listen attentively to what your subordinates and inferiors tell you. With their cooperation, you may go a long way. Your plans and ideas will be realized if you work with younger people. You will have success in radio, television, and other show productions. If you are in a responsible position in government or business, you will be able to better control your group.

If you are a woman, you are likely to be an eye-catching glamorous beauty, a bright yellow dahlia. You will have many temptations, and unless you watch out, you may get used to luxury and fall in trouble with men. You may also suffer malice from jealous people.

Other unfavorable possibilities include housing problems and quarrels between parents and children.

In a love affair or marriage proposal, there may be a change of heart.

GENERAL: Proceed aggressively. You are still somewhat dissatisfied. But don't be impatient since your luck is on the rise.

WISHES: It will come true.

MARRIAGE: Follow the advice of your mother or other trusted woman for better results.

BIRTH: Safe. But care will be required after the confinement.

HEALTH: Beware of sicknesses due to over-excitement. Consult the doctor without delay.

NEGOTIATIONS, DISPUTES: Seek an early settlement for better results. You will be at a disadvantage if more time is lost.

TRAVELING: You will be unlucky on the trip unless it is a short one. Put it off.

MISSING PROPERTY: It has fallen into someone's hands and will not be recovered if found.

AWAITED PERSONS, MESSAGES: Coming.

MONEY: You will draw on your savings. Loans will be obtained after repeated efforts.

MARKET: If the market is currently balanced at a low level, it will rise sharply and then fall a little. The trend is upward.

INDEX VARIATIONS:

1st place: Chi-Sui-Shi . . . . ●●●●○●
2nd place: Chi-Rai-Fuku . . . . ●●●●●○

CHI-KA-MEI-I

3rd place: Chi-Ten-Tai .... ●●●○○○
4th place: Rai-Taku-Ki-Mai .... ●●○●○○
5th place: Sui-Taku-Setsu ...... ●○●●○○
6th place: San-Taku-Son ...... ○●●●○○

59. Chi-Ka-Mei-I

●●● ○●○ Light Fell.

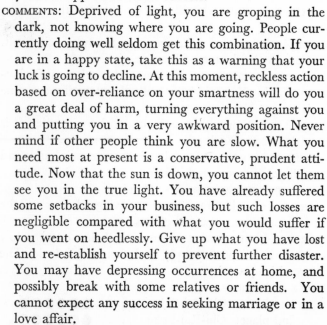

BOOK OF CHANGES: The sun is down and you are in darkness. Wait patiently until light breaks again. A new day will bring you new opportunities for success.

COMMENTS: Deprived of light, you are groping in the dark, not knowing where you are going. People currently doing well seldom get this combination. If you are in a happy state, take this as a warning that your luck is going to decline. At this moment, reckless action based on over-reliance on your smartness will do you a great deal of harm, turning everything against you and putting you in a very awkward position. Never mind if other people think you are slow. What you need most at present is a conservative, prudent attitude. Now that the sun is down, you cannot let them see you in the true light. You have already suffered some setbacks in your business, but such losses are negligible compared with what you would suffer if you went on heedlessly. Give up what you have lost and re-establish yourself to prevent further disaster. You may have depressing occurrences at home, and possibly break with some relatives or friends. You cannot expect any success in seeking marriage or in a love affair.

If you are a woman, you are likely to have a broken heart unless you are willing to be a mistress. Do you love him so much? And can you believe he loves you as much?

On spiritual matters not involving material considerations, you will not be so unlucky. In serious academic research or other unpretentious mental work, your steady efforts at this time will add up to bring you much fame some day.

In any case, you are advised to be conservative in everything, and persevere whatever happens until the time comes for you to start again. When winter comes, spring is not far off. A change for the better will come in two months or more.

GENERAL: You may make a mistake by taking a favorable view of what others say or do, and you may fall in trouble unless you refrain from imprudent talk. Beware of women.

WISHES: It will not be realized due to some obstruction.

MARRIAGE: The proposal sounds attractive but will not bear fruit.

BIRTH: Safe. The baby may be a little sickly.

HEALTH: Something terrible may happen if you are imprudent.

NEGOTIATIONS, DISPUTES: You are at a disadvantage.

TRAVELING: Beware of thieves and fires.

MISSING PROPERTY: It was stolen and will not be recovered.

MONEY: You will lose money. No loans will be obtained for the moment.

MARKET: A brief lull will be followed by a sharp fall.

INDEX VARIATIONS:

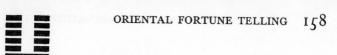

CHI-RAI-FUKU

1st place:	Chi-Zan-Ken	●●●○●●
2nd place:	Chi-Ten-Tai	●●●○○○
3rd place:	Chi-Rai-Fuku	●●●●●○
4th place:	Rai-Ka-Ho	●●○○●○
5th place:	Sui-Ka-Ki-Sai	●○●○●○
6th place:	San-Ka-Hi	○●●○●○

60. Chi-Rai-Fuku

●●● ●●○ A New Beginning.

BOOK OF CHANGES: Exhaustion and revival repeat themselves in an endless cycle. You are in a state full of youthful vigor for revival, waiting for the return of spring.

COMMENTS: This combination symbolizes November. No matter what you do, seasons return regularly every year. Despite all your present difficulties and suffering, happiness will return to you if only you remain faithful, sincere, and hard-working. People will come and help you as you become increasingly luckier. But impatience will lead to failure. Always proceed in good order. If something offends you, tolerate it for seven days, and you will have unexpected happy results. As the combination has affinity to the number "7", you may assume a cycle of seven days, seven weeks, or seven months.

There will be a "return" in anything you do. If you are starting a new project or a new business, plan it very carefully. Otherwise you will soon be "returning" where you started. If you are a woman, you may "return" from your husband to your native home.

On the other hand, a separated man and wife may come to live together again or the man who has left you in anger (if you are a woman) may come back to apologize; or an old business associate may propose to work with you again.

In any case, you will do increasingly better as you go on.

GENERAL: Your luck is on the rise, and the gloom around you is beginning to clear up. You must have already noted signs of your growing luck. Hold on a little while.

WISHES: You are in Heaven's favor. Everything will go well.

MARRIAGE: You will have success if you are marrying for the second time. If it is going to be your first marriage, the second proposal should be accepted.

BIRTH: A boy will be born safe.

HEALTH: An old ailment may return.

NEGOTIATIONS, DISPUTES: Patient effort will bring about a favorable settlement.

TRAVELING: Go on the trip with a companion.

MISSING PROPERTY: It will be found under a pile of other things.

MONEY: You will make money little by little, and it will accumulate.

MARKET: There will be a return. A high market will slump back; a low market will swing up again.

INDEX VARIATIONS:

1st place:	Kon-I-Chi	●●●●●●
2nd place:	Chi-Taku-Rin	●●●●○○
3rd place:	Chi-Ka-Mei-I	●●●○●○
4th place:	Shin-I-Rai	●●○●●○
5th place:	Sui-Rai-Chun........	●○●●●○

CHI-FU-SHO

6th place: San-Rai-I .... ○●●●●○
61. Chi-Fu-Sho ●●● ○○● Up the Ladder.

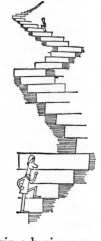

BOOK OF CHANGES: A seed long buried underground is budding vigorously to see the light of day. Youthful enthusiasm to push up is the keynote of your present state.

COMMENTS: The combination foretells growth, ascendancy, or promotion. The young plant is not well-rooted yet and vulnerable to the effects of wind and rain, but it is growing fast to become a big tree. If you are faithful to your superiors and seniors, you will be promoted without fail. With your luck steadily rising, you may begin a business on a small scale and gradually expand it until you make a fortune out of it. This, however, does not apply to speculation or gambling. Impatient moves to achieve success at a dash will produce nothing but troubles, which in turn will hinder your progress and reduce the chances of realizing your goal.

This is no time for you to start a new business on borrowed money. Use your own capital. High interest on loans would heavily handicap you. Slow but steady should be your motto. Besides, a happy turn may be forthcoming within four months.

If you are a woman, you may marry a millionaire or otherwise rise to high status through marriage. In any case, you will have much luck in marrying.

You may have some trouble about your residence. The

CHI-SUI-SHI

combination also suggests an early stage of pregnancy.

GENERAL: Great success will be achieved if you proceed carefully. You will get a promotion or a pay raise in the near future. Going ahead will bring you more luck than turning back, and you will have much luck in a game. But don't go too far. Stop at about eighty percent of your goal.

WISHES: It will come true if you wait.

MARRIAGE: It will be a good match.

BIRTH: A girl will be born safe.

HEALTH: The patient will get better, though slowly. Beware of pimples, erruptions, and skin allergy.

NEGOTIATIONS, DISPUTES: You will succeed by going ahead. An intermediary will help.

TRAVELING: The trip will be safe and pleasant. If you are going abroad, you will hear good news on the way.

MISSING PROPERTY: It will be found after some time.

AWAITED PERSONS, MESSAGES: Coming soon.

MONEY: Money will come in smoothly. Ideas and information you happen to get will bring you money, possibly in the form of brokerage.

MARKET: A gradual rise will continue fairly long.

INDEX VARIATIONS:

1st place:	Chi-Ten-Tai	●●●○○○
2nd place:	Chi-Zan-Ken	●●●○●●
3rd place:	Chi-Sui-Shi	●●●●○●
4th place:	Rai-Fu-Ko	●●○○○●
5th place:	Sui-Fu-Sei	●○●●○●
6th place:	San-Pu-Ko	○●●●○●

62. Chi-Sui-Shi ●●● ●○● War.

BOOK OF CHANGES: War, or strife among many people is going to occur. Generally, your luck is on the decline.

COMMENTS: It takes a great deal to fight a war. You need a strong army, powerful weapons, adequate information on preparations on both sides, and wise, brave decisions at critical moments. All this does not necessarily win the war. There may be unexpected developments, and in some cases you have to fight even though you know you are at a disadvantage. Life is war, a continuous series of hard battles that you must fight with all your might for survival. In a situation apparently unfavorable to you, you will wish to grasp a chance, however slim, for a miraculous victory. And such a chance comes up right in the middle of the battle. At this moment, you are like a general going to war, with all sorts of dangers and difficulties awaiting him. It is important for you now to proceed prudently, refraining from rash action, thinking well what results will be produced by the move you have in mind. Don't start shooting until the right moment comes. Hastiness will bring disaster to other people on your side as well as to yourself.

The combination predicts something different if you are a leader—a company executive, a shop proprietor, a manager, or the like. What you should do as the leader of your group is to obtain capable assistants you can really count on. If you have to fight a battle anyway, it had better be a big fight. Mobilize all men under your command and fight it out. If you are prepared to take the consequences, you are likely to see yourself through the war.

If you are a woman, you are probably cut out for business; better suited to work outside than inside the house. You are bossy, passionate, impetuous, a little capricious, and perhaps too versatile. You cannot keep in your mind what you think and feel, and have created many enemies on that account. Your sprawling battle lines need some reduction at this moment, and you need a good chief-of-staff, preferably a man.

Whether you are a man or a woman, you seem to be very active in love affairs, which are battles in a way.

GENERAL: You will attack others or be attacked by them. You are lucky and active, but beset with dangers. You may be recommended to the status of a chief or a chairman.

WISHES: Despite initial difficulty, it will be realized eventually.

MARRIAGE: Don't marry the person. You will have constant fights if you do. But if you are marrying for the second time, you may look forward to happiness.

BIRTH: The delivery will be a hard battle.

HEALTH: You are in danger. If you drive, be careful not to cause traffic accidents. You may suffer from diarrhea or neuralgia.

NEGOTIATIONS, DISPUTES: Proceed with a cool head. You will lose if you get excited.

TRAVELING: Cancel the trip.

MISSING PROPERTY: It will not be recovered, or you will find it broken.

AWAITED PERSONS, MESSAGES: Coming by surprise.

MONEY: Money will come and go swiftly, and there will be quarrels. Generally, you tend to spend much.

MARKET: There will be ups and downs due to maneuvering.

INDEX VARIATIONS:

1st place: Chi-Taku-Rin . . . . ●●●●○○

CHI-ZAN-KEN

2nd place:	Kon-I-Chi	●●●●●●
3rd place:	Chi-Fu-Sho	●●●○○●
4th place:	Rai-Sui-Kai	●●○●○●
5th place:	Kan-I-Sui	●○●●○●
6th place:	San-Sui-Mo	○●●●○●

63. Chi-Zan-Ken ●●● ○●● **Popular With Women.**

BOOK OF CHANGES: A compressed spring is bound to extend. Modesty will bring you much popularity. Your luck is moderately good.

COMMENTS: With modesty and condescension, you will live in peace and win the favor of people around you, and eventually you will head them.

Currently you may be doing rather poorly, wrestling with many problems and living on an inadequate income. But a happy break is forthcoming. You will have more luck on spiritual rather than material matters.

If you are a woman, you particularly need modesty and condescension. People around you think you are too proud and are talking about a boycott against you. With your brain, you ought to be able to change the atmosphere somehow. Follow the advice of a confidant. It is not difficult. You have only to show that you can bow. If you take the right approach, the situation will be completely changed within two months. Besides, this combination suggests male nudity. If you are a man, you are likely to be in a fix because of your complicated relations with women.

GENERAL: There is a lack of teamwork. Perhaps you should yield a little. That will make everything go smoothly again.

WISHES: It will be realized if you get the help of other people.

KON-I-CHI

MARRIAGE: Give a free hand to a trusted senior. You will be happily married.

BIRTH: Safe.

HEALTH: Beware of venereal diseases and other troubles affecting the lower half of your body.

NEGOTIATIONS, DISPUTES: Don't be too aggressive if you want to make a good deal. For better results, ask an intermediary to step in.

TRAVELING: The trip will be safe, but you had better return home soon.

MISSING PROPERTY: It will be found in the east or north, or it is hidden under some other object.

AWAITED PERSONS, MESSAGES: Coming late.

MONEY: You will be luckier in the future. For a loan, ask an old man or woman.

MARKET: Down.

INDEX VARIATIONS:

1st place:	Chi-Ka-Mei-I	●●●○●○
2nd place:	Chi-Fu-Sho	●●●○○●
3rd place:	Kon-I-Chi	●●●●●●
4th place:	Rai-San-Sho-Ka	●●○○●●'
5th place:	Sui-Zan-Ken	●○●○●●
6th place:	Gon-I-Zan	○●●○●●

64. Kon-I-Chi ●●● ●●● —Femininity.

BOOK OF CHANGES: This combination is all negative. In Yi augury, negative means feminine. With feminine perseverance, you are waiting for the coming of spring. If you are unselfish, industrious and obedient, you may look forward to much happiness and success.

COMMENTS: Winter landscape is desolate and forlorn, with few signs of life anywhere on the hills or in the fields. But soon spring will be here with its flowers and singing birds. All your hardship and suffering will come to an end in just two months, and you will be rewarded handsomely for your present patience and effort. Don't turn back halfway. The summit is in sight.

You are often so eager for material gains that you fail to respect established moral standards, and when you cannot have your own way in anything, you tend to behave stubbornly. You will do much better if you reflect on these weaknesses of yours. Happiness will come to you when you have learned to cooperate with others in a faithful, friendly manner. For assistance, turn to someone in the southwest, or to an old woman.

If you are a man, you are probably serious-minded, introspective, and strongly attached to your mother. Perhaps you are a little feminine and delicate. You are cut out for clerical work rather than for straight business, and will make a good internal worker rather than a field salesman.

If you are a woman, you are probably pretty with a tendency to stubbornness. You stand a good chance of marrying happily.

GENERAL: Patience and hard work will bring you recognition and success.

Restrain your desire for material gains.

WISHES: It will not be realized immediately due to some difficulty.

MARRIAGE: It is an ideal match. But don't hurry. Impatience will breed trouble.

BIRTH: Safe. Good care should be taken after the confinement.

HEALTH: Beware of illnesses affecting your digestive organs or a liver disease due to fatigue. Once contracted, such an illness will persist.

TRAVELING: You had better put off the trip unless you are going with a group.

MISSING PROPERTY: It will not be found immediately.

AWAITED PERSONS, MESSAGES: Coming soon. The person is interested in you.

MONEY: Your efforts will pay off.

MARKET: Down.

INDEX VARIATIONS:

1st place:	Chi-Rai-Fuku.........	●●●●●○
2nd place:	Chi-Sui-Shi..........	●●●●○●
3rd place:	Chi-Zan-Ken	●●●○●●
4th place:	Rai-Chi-Yo..........	●●○●●●
5th place:	Sui-Chi-Hi	●○●●●●
6th place:	San-Chi-Haku	○●●●●●

Chapter Three

Turn a Misfortune Into a Blessing

LOOKING over these descriptions of the sixty-four Yi combinations, you will note that few of them promise you unconditional good luck, telling you that you can do whatever you like regardless of where you stand.

Yi augury is based on common sense. Of course, there are miraculous changes in life, but they do not occur normally. It is unlikely that you should wake up to find yourself a millionaire, and the course of history seldom changes overnight. Careful analysis will show that such a change comes as a result of many forces that have been at work for a long time, and that there have been signs foretelling it.

When you turn to Yi augury, more often than not you are not in a happy state, having a problem or a complaint, or wondering about something. You have something weighing on your mind. "It will be all right again tomorrow," you tell yourself, but such wishful thinking often disappoints you. Yi augury tells you exactly what is wrong with you, and you can eliminate the cause of trouble it points out. Many people, however, are too lazy to do so. Instead, they want to know what will happen in the next phase of their future, and Yi augury's answer to that question cannot be a favorable one, naturally.

Others want to know what should be done to put an

end to the present spell of bad luck. But it is part of the general pattern of your fortune, which changes in a cycle. The bad spell may be shortened by eliminating the basic cause of trouble, but it cannot be terminated at once and replaced by a new period of good luck. An onset of bad luck, once started, will continue until it runs itself out, and it is no use complaining about it. The important thing to do is to find out how long it will last, and that depends on where you stand in your cycle of good and bad luck.

If you get an unfavorable answer when you are in difficulty, don't lose hope or act recklessly in desperation, for Yi angury never leaves you in a totally hopeless state. There is always a way out. Personally, the author thinks much of a turning point in Fortune's wheel. A change for the better is bound to come in any situation. The question is, how soon? The answer will be provided by your index number, which also tells you the pattern of change.

Among variations of Yi augury are physiogenomy (dealing with your features), chiromancy (palm-reading), aspect divination (dealing with directions), onomancy (dealing with names), astrology, seal divination, and grave divination. The author would recommend a combination of physiognomy, palm-reading, and bowel-movement divination, for these strongly reflect your vitality.

Every morning, before washing your face, look at yourself in the mirror. If you are in adversity, you will probably look pale and sickly. On the other hand, if you are full of vitality with your luck rising, your complexion is likely to be healthy and youthful, and your bowel movement will be favorable accordingly. By the same token, constipation spells bad luck. As for chiromancy, if your palm is sanguine and tense with the lines showing clearly, it may be considered to have vitality, indicating that you will soon be out of the crisis or difficulty you are now in, possibly with the help of someone.

It is only natural that you should get a poor combination of elements when you are in trouble. But if you note encouraging signs in these three aspects of your physical condition, you may assume that there will soon be a happy break in the long spell of bad luck.

The most important thing you can learn from Yi augury is the time of the next turn in your cycle of luck, and no matter how poorly you are doing, there is always a chance of escape.

Yi augurs in the past have relied chiefly on the statistical approach, i.e., simulating the future on the analysis of the past. The philosophy underlying this book is less fatalistic, for it advises you to let by-gones be by-gones and concentrate on discovering where you stand at present in order to find how you can improve your present situation and achieve greater success and happiness.

Yi augury provides a vital key to your future.

Other TUT BOOKS available: